Hellenic Studies 71

THE *AETHIOPIS*

Recent Titles in the Hellenic Studies Series

THE *AETHIOPIS*

Neo-Neoanalysis Reanalyzed

by
Malcolm Davies

Center for Hellenic Studies
Trustees for Harvard University
Washington, DC
Distributed by Harvard University Press
Cambridge, Massachusetts, and London, England
2016

The Aethiopis: Neo-Neoanalysis Reanalyzed
    By Malcolm Davies
Copyright © 2016 Center for Hellenic Studies, Trustees for Harvard University
All Rights Reserved.
Published by Center for Hellenic Studies, Trustees for Harvard University,
    Washington, D.C.
Distributed by Harvard University Press, Cambridge, Massachusetts and
    London, England
Printed by Edwards Brothers Malloy, Ann Arbor, MI and Lillington, NC
Cover Design: Joni Godlove
Production: Kerri Cox Sullivan

Library of Congress Cataloging-in-Publication Data

Davies, Malcolm, 1951– author.
  The Aethiopis : neo-neoanalysis reanalyzed / by Malcolm Davies.
      pages   cm. — (Hellenic studies ; 71)
  Includes bibliographical references and index.
  ISBN 978-0-674-08831-3 (alk. paper)
1. Aethiopis. 2. Epic poetry, Greek—History and criticism.   I. Title. II. Series:
Hellenic studies ; 71.

PA3873.A95A6233 2015
883'.01—dc23   2015032442

For
Martin West
In memoriam

Contents

Preface

HEREWITH THE NEXT INSTALLMENT OF MY SERIES of commentaries on early epic fragments (for details see the preface to the first volume, *The Theban Epics*, which appeared in 2014). The following volume, dealing with the *Cypria*, will be the longest so far, and the present volume easily the shortest, and it will be worth the while briefly to consider why this should be. The number of fragments that can be assigned to the *Aethiopis* even on the most generous estimate (which I do not share) is extremely small, although we do have Proclus' prose summary of its contents to establish a narrative framework. The world will have to wait, however impatiently, for my general views on the origins and reliability of that summary until they appear, as their most logical position requires, in the later volume embracing the *Titanomachy*, first poem of the Epic Cycle. Until then, there are reliable introductions to this issue available in, for instance, the relevant monographs by Burgess and West as listed in my bibliography. The considerations which make the so-considerably lost epic worth studying in a separate, if small, monograph are twofold. First, the possibility, long entertained by a number of scholars, that its contents in some way influenced the plot of parts of the *Iliad*, Second, the possibility that certain vase paintings reflect the versions of events displayed in the *Aethiopis*. This latter interface between art and literature, looming large also in the case of Stesichorus, has always fascinated me, and the chapter devoted to it here may be regarded as a down payment on a larger and future study of the more general issue. The former consideration brings us to the topic known as Neoanalysis. This already-controversial topic has been further complicated by the advent of the oral theory in Homeric studies, and scholarly opinions have veered for and against (and back again) in a not-altogether predictable manner. My first chapter here endeavors to give a dispassionate account of the history of the debate, its present state, and the balance of probabilities as they strike me.

As with my previous volume on the Theban epics, earlier drafts of this book were read and improved by Hugh Lloyd-Jones and Rudolf Kassel. Appropriately, given the above mentioned relevance of vase paintings, a draft was also read and improved by John Boardman. Martin West, who looked at a final draft of the Theban volume, was prevented by his sudden and untimely death from so benefiting the present book. I have, of course, profited from the relevant portion of his monograph on the Epic Cycle, and my occasional disagreements over details will disguise from the percipient neither this fact nor my sense of this loss to the classical and, indeed, academic world at large. I dedicate this book to his memory.[1]

---

[1] Given the large number of forthcoming studies on the issue of (Neo-)neoanalysis, I shall be returning to the topic and its significance for the *Aethiopis* in a not altogether inappropriate place: the end of the commentary on the *Cypria* mentioned above.

Abbreviations of Frequently Cited Works

ABV	J. D. Beazley, *Attic Black-Figure Vase-Painters* (Oxford 1956).
ANRW	H. Temporini, ed., *Aufstieg und Niedergang der römischen Welt* (Berlin 1972–).
ARV²	J. D. Beazley, *Attic Red-Figure Vase-Painters*, 2nd ed. (Oxford 1963).
CB	L. D. Caskey and J. D. Beazley, *Attic Vase Paintings in the Museum of Fine Arts Boston* 2 (Oxford 1954); 3 (Boston 1963).
GGL	L. Schmid, *Geschichte der griechischen Literatur*, vol. 1.1 (Munich 1929).
Gruppe, *Gr. Myth.*	O. Gruppe, *Griechische Mythologie und Religionsgeschichte*, 2 vols. (Munich 1906).
Heldensage	C. Robert, *Die griechische Heldensage*, vol. 2 (Berlin 1920).
LIMC	*Lexicon Iconographicum Mythorum Classicorum* (Zurich and Munich 1981–1999).
LSJ	H. G. Liddell, R. Scott, and H. S. Jones, *Greek-English Lexicon*, 9th ed. (Oxford 1940).
MW	R. Merkelbach and M. L. West, *Hesiodi Fragmenta* (Oxford 1967).
Pfister-Roesgen	G. Pfister-Roesgen, *Die etruskischen Spiegel des 5. Jhs. v. Chr.* (*Archäologische Studien* 2 [1975]).

PMGF	*Poetarum Melicorum Graecorum Fragmenta,* vol. I: *Alcman Stesichorus Ibycus. Post D. L. Page,* ed. Malcolm Davies (Oxford 1991).
RE	*Real-Enzyklopädie des Klassischen Altertumswissenschaft* (1893).
Roscher	W. H. Roscher, *Ausführliches Lexikon der griechischen und römischen Mythologie* (Leipzig 1884).
TrGF	*Tragicorum Graecorum Fragmenta,* ed. B. Snell, S. Radt, and R. Kannicht (Göttingen 1971–2004).

van Thiel = Helmut van Thiel, *Aristarch, Aristophanes Byzantios, Demetrios Ixion, Zenodot: Fragmente zur Ilias gesammelt, neu herausgegeben und kommentiert* (Berlin 2014).

Vian, Budé text Quintus of Smyrna = F. Francis Vian, *Quintus de Smyrne: La Suite d'Homère. Texte établi et traduit.* Tome i *(Livres i–iv)* (Collection Budé) (Paris 1963). Tome ii *(Livres v–ix)* (Collection Budé) (Paris 1966).

Wilamowitz, *Glaube der Hellenen* = Ulrich von Wilamowitz, *Der Glaube der Hellenen* (Berlin 1931).

Wilamowitz, *Ilias und Homer* = Ulrich von Wilamowitz, *Die Ilias und Homer* (Berlin 1916).

Introduction

"WE KNOW LESS ABOUT THIS POEM THAN WE THINK WE DO" would, of course, be a suitable cautionary rubric for most, if not all, of the works contained within the Epic Cycle. But it seems to me to apply with a particular appropriateness to the *Aethiopis*, a composition from which, contrary to initial impressions, we possess no securely attested direct citation—indeed only one indubitable fragment of any sort, and that from a portion of the poem which falls outside the scope of Proclus' résumé (on which see pages 45–81 below). The evidence of art has been thought to expand the range of remarks we can safely make about the work's contents: so it does, but its aid too sometimes proves delusive.

Our knowledge of the poem is not so circumscribed that we cannot dispense, right at the start, with one or two totally implausible conjectures concerning its structure and origins. It was only to be expected that at the height of the craze for Analysis our epic too should be subjected to the strains and tensions undergone by extant compositions. If the *Odyssey* could be resolved into such constituent elements as *Telemachy*, *Nekyia*, *Return*, and the like, which once existed as independent epics in their own right, did not the *Aethiopis* represent an amalgamation of two distinct poems, a *Penthesileid* and a *Memnonid* as it might be, which were run together under the supervision of some later mind? The existence of a tradition that attributed an *Amazonia* to Homer bestowed a supposititious plausibility upon this reconstruction (cf. *Suda s.v.* "Homer" [3.526 Adler]). Rzach in his *RE* article (1922:2399.32–50) provides a convenient summary of the views of scholars who concur in positing an independent *Memnonid* or the like.[1]

Alexandre Severyns, in his important article "L'*Éthiopide* d'Arctinos et la question du Cycle épique" (1925) sought to bring order and reason into what he with justice called this "chaos des épopées." In the first place, there is simply no

---

[1]   But C. A. Lobeck (*Aglaophamus* [Königsberg 1829] 1.417–418) should not be cited (as he is by A. Severyns, "L'*Éthiopide* d'Arctinos et la question du Cycle épique," *Révue de Philologie* 49 [1925]: 154) as believing that "l'*Amazonie* homérique ne différait pas de la *Penthésileide* d'Arctinos." All Lobeck infers from the variant last line of the *Iliad* is that it was intended to link *Amazonia* and *Iliad*.

ancient evidence for any such multiplicity of sources for our poem, and no argument by analogy should be allowed. The futility of speculation upon the alleged prehistory of the *Iliad* or the *Odyssey* was well exposed by G. S. Kirk (*The Songs of Homer* [Cambridge 1962] 228–229), even though the existence of some sort of prehistory can hardly be denied.[2]

When the supposed end product of the process thus extrapolated has disappeared to the extent the *Aethiopis* has suffered, the sheer pointlessness of hypothesizing earlier forms must be apparent to all. Then again, the very notion that a separate poem ever existed whose sole subject matter was the career of a single Amazon, a figure who is accorded a very secondary role within the story of Achilles, is far less likely than many dissectors have allowed. That the episodes involving Memnon bulked larger in the epic as a whole must have struck the person responsible for devising its present title. Furthermore, as Robert (*Heldensage* 2.1175–1176) has pointed out, the *Aethiopis* seems to have displayed some kind of symmetry in its plot: two major allies come to help Priam and are killed by Achilles; these are Penthesileia, from the north, and Memnon, from the south, both (in strong contrast to the Trojan allies of the *Iliad*) dwelling in remote fantasy lands.[3] It rather looks as if Penthesileia and Memnon were early conceived as a corresponding pair.

---

[2]   West (2013:135) has reintroduced, if not chaos, at least the issue of prehistory, with his theory that the *Aethiopis* was "constituted from two independent pieces of composition, an *Amazonis* and a *Memnonis*." This notion seems to rest largely on his observation (133) that the episode of Penthesileia does nothing to advance the plot, indeed merely—by complicating it with the interlude of Thesites' death and its consequences—delays its climax, the death of Achilles. But such retardation is the very stuff of Cyclic epic: think of how the *Cypria* sets back the arrival at Troy by the devices of the Teuthranian expedition and the delay at Aulis. Think of the *Ilias Parva*'s fetching of first Neoptolemus and then Philoctetes to Troy, and the need to steal the Palladium, all of which delay the climactic sack of the city. Retardation is not even unknown to the *Iliad*: compare e.g. the role of Diomedes in postponing the revival of Trojan fortunes. For other aspects of West's theory see page 23 below.

[3]   On the "geometrical symmetries" by which the *Aethiopis* (in contrast to Homer's epics) seems to have been partly ordered see further J. B. Hainsworth, "Joining Battle in Homer," *Greece and Rome* 13 (1966): 159.

Chapter 1

The *Aethiopis* and the *Iliad*

T HE PLOTS OF MANY AN EPIC HAVE BEEN RECONSTITUTED from alleged references and allusions in Homer (this is particularly true of the *Thebais*). The *Aethiopis*, however, occupies a special position among these. An examination of this position must take us into the realms of Neoanalysis—magical name and concept, which has seemed to some scholars to open the doors to important and profound truths about Homer and the Epic Cycle, although by others it is condemned as the product of flawed logic and a misapprehension as to the manner in which early epics are likely to have influenced each other.

That the scene in *Iliad* VIII where Diomedes rescues Nestor from Hector is modeled on a similar scene in the *Aethiopis*—in which Antilochus rescued Nestor from Memnon—was already asserted by Welcker (2:174).[1] A more general theory of the *Aethiopis* as prior to and model for the *Iliad* may be found as early as Bethe (1922), for instance, or Severyns (1925:167n1; for a summary, with bibliography, of the basic suppositions of more recent adherents, see West 2003:4–6 = 2011:247–249), but the basic texts of Neoanalysis proper were, to my mind, four: Heinrich Pestalozzi, *Die Achilleis als Quelle der Ilias* (Erlenbach 1945); J. Th. Kakridis, *Homeric Researches* (Lund 1949) 65–95; Wolfgang Schadewaldt, *Varia Variorum: Festgabe für K. Reinhardt* (Münster 1952) 13–48 = *Von Homers Welt und Werk*[4] (Leipzig 1965) 155–202; and Georg Schoeck, *Ilias und Aethiopis: Kyklische Motive in homerischer Brechung* (Zurich 1961). These scholars also provide further references to earlier works (by themselves and other writers) along the same lines, and the bibliography may be rendered fuller still by an examination of the detailed and sympathetic accounts of Neoanalyst views on the *Aethiopis* in various studies by Wolfgang Kullmann, the most persistent defender and refiner

---

[1] See West 2003:1–4 = 2011:242–247 for a summary of other, even earlier, pre-Neoanalytic views that presuppose the *Aethiopis* as model for the *Iliad*. On the *Thebais* see M. Davies, *The Theban Epics* (Washington 2014) 32–40.

of these views in modern times. Note especially (1) this scholar's *Die Quellen der Ilias: Troischer Sagenkreis* (Wiesbaden 1960) 30–51, which endeavors to answer the objections raised by two formidably probing reviews of Neoanalyst theory (that of Pestalozzi's book by F. Focke ["Homerisches," *La Nouvelle Clio* 3 (1951): 335–338], and that of Schadewaldt's by Uvo Hölscher [*Gnomon* 27 (1955): 385–399]); (2) his remarks in *Gnomon* 49 (1977): 529–543 = *Homerische Motive: Beiträge zur Entstehung, Eigenart und Wirkung von Ilias und Odyssee* (Stuttgart 1992) 198–215 (in a review of the book by Dihle mentioned below), where he attempts to reformulate in more precise terms his and other scholars' Neoanalytical ideas in order to combat more recent criticisms of them; and (3) his "Zur Methode der Neoanalyse in der Homerforschung," *Wiener Studien* 15 (1981): 5–42 = *Homerische Motive*, 67–99, which takes the apologia and refinement still further, and prefaces them with a useful prehistory of Neoanalysis.

Let us turn to the more recent criticisms. Of those published in Germany I name but two:[2] Albin Lesky in the new *Pauly-Wissowa* article *s.v.* "Homeros" (*RE* Suppl. 11 [Stuttgart 1968]) has a useful discussion of the problems involved (and a rich bibliography) in cols. 757–764 = 71–78 *Sonderdruck* (Stuttgart 1967). I quote throughout from the latter. And Albrecht Dihle offers a penetrating examination of Neoanalytical assumptions (especially those of Schadewaldt [1952]) in the first chapter of his *Homer-Probleme* (Cologne 1970).[3] On the whole, his conclusions are very skeptical. English scholars have as a rule reacted with hostility to the approach under discussion. A particularly extreme example is D. L. Page's review of Schoeck's book ("Homer and the Neoanalytiker," *Classical Review* 13 [1963]: 21–24), a devastating onslaught upon "the procedures and principles" of what Page terms "this small but expanding circle."

Far more discriminating are the comments of M. M. Willcock ("The Funeral Games of Patroclus," *Bulletin of the Institute of Classical Studies* 20 [1973]: 4–9). His stress upon the *complexity* of the issues involved is particularly timely, and I myself am particularly concerned to associate myself with this emphasis here, since I will now proceed to summarize some of the questions at stake and, as Kullmann (1977:533 = *Homerische Motive*, 202) has pointed out, such summaries are not best calculated to convey complexities of this nature.

---

[2]   Reinhardt's posthumously published book *Die Ilias und ihr Dichter* (Göttingen 1961) is hard to categorize in this context. He argues against the *Aethiopis* theory (349–337) but is generally Neoanalytical in outlook. As Kullmann says in his review of Reinhardt's section on this topic (*Göttingische Gelehrte Anzeigen* 217 [1965]): 25 = *Homerische Motive*, 186) "Die Übereinstimmungen mit Schadewaldt und Pestalozzi sind größer als die Divergenzen."

[3]   For further bibliography see Kelly 2006:1n1, 2nn2, 4; Burgess 2001:61–64 is particularly good.

Iliad VIII 80–129

I begin with the oldest and firmest link in the theory, what even the hostile Page acknowledges to be "the strongest single weapon in the whole armoury" (1963:23). A consideration of the issues raised by *Iliad* VIII 80–129 will bring us into contact with most of the problems inherent in Neoanalysis's interpretation of the various passages in question. Nestor's horse is shot by Paris, and the old man seems doomed as Hector speeds down upon him. Diomedes, however, comes to the rescue. Compare with this the scene from the *Aethiopis* as reconstituted (reasonably enough: see page 64 below) from Proclus' summary and Pindar: Nestor's horse is shot by Paris, and the old man seems doomed as Memnon speeds down upon him. Nestor's son Antilochus comes to the rescue, however, and saves his father at the cost of his own life: for Memnon kills him and is in turn himself killed by Achilles.

I do not think any scholar has seriously tried to deny the obvious similarities between the two scenes. Difficulties come crowding on us thick and fast, however, when we try to decide just how to interpret these similarities.

Interdependence of Original and Copy

Perhaps one scene is modeled on the other. If so, which came first? The majority of scholars have argued for the priority of the *Aethiopis*'s version,[4] because "since here the rescuer is the rescued's own son, himself to be killed by the attacker" (Page 1963:23) this version seems more basic, more organic, more integral, more tragic,[5] to its story.[6] But we have not advanced very far and are already confronted by two enormous and momentous issues of principle. First of all, is it really the case that a motif's superior relevance to its context is to be equated so instinctively with that context's primacy?[7] Several scholars (especially Lesky [1967: 75.12–42] and Dihle [1970:12]) have done good service in stressing how a motif can be *improved* when used on a later occasion,[8] how a later poet can expand or

---

[4] For bibliography see West 2003:10 = 2010:256n65. Schadewaldt (1952:97n2) is the main exception: he believes the reverse process would be equally possible. So, too, does Hölscher (1955:392) assert the *Iliad*'s priority.

[5] For further consideration of this criterion see page 10 below.

[6] Note, too (with Andersen [1978:113]), that Nestor's plight as here depicted has no parallel anywhere else within the *Iliad*.

[7] "'Gut ist alt' und 'jung ist schlect' als prinzipelle," as Lesky (*RE* 8^A [1934]: 1249–1250) has wittily expressed it.

[8] To say nothing of the likelihood that one and the same poet may adapt motifs from one and the same source effectively in one place and indifferently in another (cf. Dodds 1968:34n47, though I do not accept his view that *Iliad* VIII 80–129 is one such example of "clumsy adaptation": see page 8n13 below).

correct an earlier work's application of a motif, so that abbreviated or seemingly inferior employment of a motif is no necessary sign of relative lateness.

And we are not yet finished with this first problem. For I have just raised a further issue in referring to "seemingly inferior employment of a motif." Kullmann has complained (1960:36 and 39 in particular: the complaint is largely aimed at Hölscher [1955]) that opponents of Neoanalysis sometimes behave as if they had securely established the principle that where a motif is employed in a satisfactory enough way, there is no need to search for any model or precedent.

The responsibility for this largely rests with those Neoanalysts who have sought to promulgate their cause by exaggerating and overestimating the number of oddities and anomalies in a given scene in order to establish (often in an uncharacteristically insensitive and philistine manner[9]) its inferiority relative to the alleged "source." This way of proceeding—aptly summed up by Kelly (2006:12) as a "search for difficulties"—leaves no alternative to opponents but to demolish the hypothesis by showing that, on the contrary, the features of the scene in question are perfectly acceptable, and often magnificently effective, as literature. It will be as well to establish at once what has been very well formulated: "Zeitliche Priorität eines Textes im Vergleich zu einem anderen, der dasselbe Motiv verwendet, ist nicht maßgeblich für ein Urteil über seinen poetischen Wert" (Ø. Andersen, *Die Diomedesgestalt in der Ilias* [*Symbolae Osloenses* Suppl. 25 (1978)] 118).

It remains true that this type of counterargument does not logically exclude the possibility that the relevant passage still had a source in the *Aethiopis*. But Neoanalysts must accept that this possibility is not susceptible of proof, and that their position here is nowhere near as secure as in those few cases where they can point to genuinely puzzling features.

Superior and inferior uses of a motif are no magic key to relative dating, then. Another possible key: "If there are two uses of a motif, one tragic the other not, then the tragic version must be primary and original." This handy rule, formulated by Kullmann (1960:58–63 and 1981:11, 19, 25–26 = *Homerische Motive*, 72, 79, 85–86; and independently by Reinhardt [1961:88 and 93–94]) underlies a good deal of scholarly writing on this topic. So if Antilochus rescues Nestor but at the cost of his own life, while Diomedes does the same and survives, the former version must be the original and the second derivative. By and large I think this holds true. Of course we must remember that, by virtue of the restricted period of time covered by its subject matter, the *Iliad* can display few genuinely tragic

---

[9] A good example is Pestalozzi (1945:10), whose "imaginary problems" are well dealt with by Kelly (2006:4–5). Cf. Cook as cited below, page 8n13.

eventualities for its main heroes. Most of these must survive the poem to fulfill the mythical role allotted to them.

And some specific cases do not bear out this general principle quite as conclusively as might at first be thought: note, for instance, Andersen on the relationship between Thersites' death in the *Aethiopis*, and his drubbing in *Iliad* II: "'Abschwächung' oder 'pathetische Steigerung'—beides ist möglich" (Andersen 1982:24).

Now what precisely do we mean by "the priority of the *Aethiopis*'s version"? This sort of language has given rise to the notion that Neoanalysts "tend to argue as if there were precise and exact links, as if the *Iliad*, composed at one moment in time, was directly indebted to a particular version of the story of Memnon" (Willcock 1973:6). And this seems so obviously inadequate to the repercussions of "Milman Parry's proof that Homer's style is typical of oral poetry"[10] that a scholar with Page's gift for caustic invective can mockingly represent the Neoanalysts as "having determined that Homer composed the *Iliad* in much the same manner as Virgil composed the *Aeneid*" (21).

Dihle too (1970:9–11) interprets Neoanalysis as presupposing *written* sources for Homer. It is reassuring that Kullmann in his reply to this type of criticism denies that Neoanalysis necessarily implies such written sources and seems (now at least) fully alert to the complexities of the issues (see e.g. 1977:531 = *Homerische Motive*, 200; and 1981:9, 13, 18, 27, and 33n76 = *Homerische Motive*, 70–71, 74, 78, 86, and 91n76). So he asserts that even if the Epic Cycle is likely to be later than Homer the possibility of influence upon the *Iliad* and the *Odyssey* by earlier oral versions of these cyclic epics is not thereby excluded. And he distinguishes between the pre-Homeric *conception* of various themes and motifs and their post-Homeric *preservation in written form*.

Let us finally return to the specific instance that gave rise to this examination of principles and approaches. Are we any the better able now to decide how to interpret the similarities between the attacks launched upon Nestor by Hector and Memnon? After careful consideration, I would still follow Willcock (7)[11] and Kullmann (esp. 1977:533 = *Homerische Motive*, 202; and 1981:10 and n16 = *Homerische Motive*, 71) in maintaining that the version later preserved in the epic now known as the *Aethiopis* has a claim to the status of model for the account found in *Iliad* VIII.[12] This decision is nothing like as obvious and clear-cut as some

---

[10] The cautious formulation is owed to Gray (J. L. Myres, *Homer and His Critics*, ed. D. Gray [London 1958] 241). See A. Parry, ed., *The Making of Homeric Verse: The Collected Papers of Milman Parry* (Oxford 1971) lxin1; cf. C. W. Macleod's edition of *Iliad* XXIV (Cambridge 1982) 37n3, etc.

[11] See too his remarks in Willcock 1983:482.

[12] So too, for instance, Wilamowitz, *Ilias und Homer*, 45–46; Bethe 1922.1:111; Rzach 1922:2408–2409. Agnosticism in e.g. Vian's Budé text of Quintus Smyrnaeus (i.50n4).

of the older Neoanalysts once claimed. The *Iliad*'s version is by no means an incoherent copy, incomprehensible without reference to its "original." Willcock himself (1973) has drawn attention to the effective economy and subtlety of the Iliadic scene: "in about twenty lines, it firmly characterises five people (Paris, Nestor, Hector, Diomedes, and Odysseus)."[13] Without external evidence we should never guess that it was inspired by a scene involving Memnon, or complain (as does Kullmann [1960:32]) that the contrast in character between Diomedes and Odysseus at *Iliad* VIII 90–102 is irrelevant to the scene's main function. But such inspiration nevertheless remains the most convincing and economic explanation of the phenomena.

Antilochus, according to Kullmann (1960), is only important for the *Iliad* in those portions of the poem which on other grounds can be shown to have been modeled on the *Aethiopis* (i.e., on the material later incorporated in that epic) rather than vice versa. Willcock too (1973:7–8) is convinced that these passages are important for the theory under consideration, although he expresses himself rather more cautiously and with a greater awareness of the complex range of possibilities.

Independence of Thematically Similar Material

Some scholars might argue that the above readjustments of Neoanalytical perspectives do not go far enough. They would stress the existence of a wide range of thematic material at the poet's disposal. In such circumstances, the duplication of scenes between one epic and another, or indeed within the same epic, leads not to the deductions just considered, but to the obvious and unspecific conclusion that the Homeric poet had at his fingertips a rich resource of motifs, a fertile tradition capable of considerable flexibility.

The *typicality* of much of the contents of the *Iliad* and the *Odyssey* has received abundant attention from scholars of the past century. Their work is well analyzed and carried forward by Bernard Fenik in his important book, *Typical Battle Scenes in the Iliad* (*Hermes Einzelschriften* 21 [1968]).[14] For a particularly incisive and well-balanced treatment of the problem with which we are now concerned see his "Index of Subjects," *s.v.* "Aithiopis." In the sections there listed he manfully tackles the issue of whether interdependence or thematic resemblance better explains a passage like *Iliad* VIII 80–129. He rightly abstains from clear-cut conclusions. The evidence is too complex and ambiguous, and Fenik well conveys this situation in the following paragraph (235):

---

[13] See further Andersen 1978:114, and now the excellent treatment by E. F. Cook, "On the Importance of *Iliad* Book Eight," *Classical Philology* 104 (2009): 133–161, accepting both influence from the *Aethiopis* and full and superb integration of the passage within the *Iliad*.

[14] Compare his earlier study, *Iliad X and the Rhesus: The Myth* (*Collection Latomus* 73 [1964] 30–33).

If the typical manner of composition in the *Iliad*'s battle scenes points to the existence of a traditional, inherited style, then there is probably at least an even chance that those details which the *Iliad* and *Aethiopis* share, and which occur only once in the *Iliad*, are a result of the stylistic tradition common to both poems rather than direct borrowings by one from the other. It could, however, be objected that the theory of direct influence by the *Aethiopis* on the *Iliad*, and the evidence of typical composition in the *Iliad*, are not mutually exclusive. It is easy to imagine how a particularly good epic poem might inspire direct imitation, even though neither its plot nor its details were strikingly new or unusual—that is, did not deviate substantially from the inherited tradition. The *Iliad*'s battle scenes could thus be both entirely typical and at the same time be directly modelled at certain points on the *Aethiopis* or any other poem that had made a special impression on Homer.

And we must again commend him for the following realization that the subject is even more tangled and involved than so far allowed (236):

There is, however, still another side to the question. If the *Aethiopis* was a genuine epic poem, it must have been composed according to many of the same rules as the *Iliad* itself, since the evidence for the *Iliad* points to the existence of a collective style and a collective diction that were employed for all poems of this type. One should not, in other words, assume that the *Aethiopis* was composed according to principles that were basically different from those used in the *Iliad*, or that it was somehow more "original," or represented a first starting point and ultimate source for subsequent poetry. This means, specifically, that if the *Aethiopis* grew out of the same epic tradition as the *Iliad*, which, if older than the *Iliad*, it probably did, it was most likely as typical and as derived as the *Iliad* itself. This in turn suggests that the death of Achilles at the hands of Paris and Apollo, the siege of Troy, and so forth, were sung by other poets before the *Aethiopis* poet put his hand to the material and that Homer could therefore have heard the story in many other versions besides the *Aethiopis*. There were most likely not only traditional legends, but traditional incidents, scenes, and plots which were used over and over again. We probably come closer to the truth if we see in those incidents and details shared by the *Iliad* and *Aethiopis* not inventions by the poet of the latter, which were then copied and re-cast by Homer, or vice versa, but as typical epic material which was the sole property of no single poet or poem.

These two extracts nicely illustrate the evenly balanced state of the question.

Fenik finally decides (237) that the similarities between *Iliad* and *Aethiopis*, especially as they center around the attack on Nestor, are too great to be a matter of coincidence. Even when we remember the importance of motifs, "the evidence from the battle scenes alone will not support the conclusion that the larger elements of action and plot are also typical. Until this can be demonstrated, the formidable list of similarities between the two poems can still be taken to indicate a direct, purposeful imitation of one by the other." But then a consideration of the numerous duplicated motifs in Greek myths (the invulnerable hero, the unfaithful and/or murderous wife, and so forth) induces a further modification of his position and his last words on the subject are (239) that

> when we re-consider the *Iliad-Aethiopis* problem in this light the similarities of plot and incident between the two poems are not as unequivocal as they first appear. ... Is it not possible that wrath, abstention from battle, or vengeance for a slain friend were popular themes and the subjects for many epic poems? ... All this still does not prove that a direct relationship between the *Iliad* and *Aethiopis* does not exist, but it does show how hard it is to arrive at certain conclusions based merely on similarities between them. These similarities must be viewed against the background of an epic tradition in which myths proliferated, repetitions were popular, and doublets freely constructed. ... The similarities do exist and are important. They do not, however, point unequivocally to a simple model–copy relationship between the two poems, or even to such a subtle and complex one as Schadewaldt attempted to demonstrate.

When the case for independent use of similar motifs is so sensibly and sensitively put, its differences from the alternative mode of explaining the phenomena seem very small. For instance, in both approaches, the presence or absence of parallels from the *Iliad* itself for motifs being considered is paramount (see page 8 above). See further page 12 below.

Antilochus Elsewhere in the *Iliad*[15]

In *Iliad* V 561-573 Antilochus saves Menelaus' life by standing next to him in the battle, thus inducing the retreat of the threatening Aeneas. Kullmann sees in this a further "non-tragic" reworking of the Nestor–Memnon confrontation, analogous to what we find in *Iliad* VIII 102-129, but here it is difficult not to

---

[15] On this topic see in general M. M. Willcock, "Antilochus in the *Iliad*" (1983). For skepticism about his "special relationship" with Antilochus in the *Aethiopis*, see West 2003:10–11 = 2011:256–257 with bibliography 256n45.

listen to those scholars who stress (from slightly differing angles) the cross-references between this and other scenes in the *Iliad*. Thus Fenik observes the ample parallels this same poem provides for the pattern of Trojan retreat before a Greek warrior aiding a threatened comrade. He concludes that "the simplest and most economical explanation is that the *Iliad* scenes and the *Aethiopis* passage are examples of common type scenes that doubtless appeared in many poems and with many variations" (1968:59-60).

Willcock draws our attention to the other Iliadic passages where Antilochus and Menelaus are linked: e.g. XV 568-575, where the two warriors sally forth together, and XXIII 566-601, where the former easily and effectively quenches the rage of the latter.

In *Iliad* XVI 317-329 Thrasymedes saves his brother Antilochus when he is about to be attacked by the Trojan Maris. Again Reinhardt (1961:357) and with him Kullmann (see more recently 1981:10 = *Homerische Motive*, 71-72) detect a relationship with the *Aethiopis*, this time a *reversal* of the situation that prevailed there when Thrasymedes was unable to help his brother. But Fenik is correct (196-197) to insist: "The circumstances here are entirely different, nor is there anywhere a mention of Thrasymedes' failure to stand by his brother when Antilochus challenged Memnon." Once more the answer seems to be that this situation in *Iliad* XVI is a typical one, paralleled elsewhere in the epic.

Willcock and Kullmann are agreed that in his other Iliadic appearances Antilochus anticipates his role as a replacement for Patroclus in Achilles' affections. Few (though see 10n15 above) are likely to wish to reject this analysis when successively confronted by scenes wherein Antilochus is dispatched (by Menelaus, significantly enough) to tell Achilles the news of Patroclus' death (XVII 691-699); where he seizes Achilles' hands in case he tries to cut his own throat (XVIII 1-34); and, most striking of all, where his genial and engaging conduct at the Funeral Games of Patroclus makes Achilles smile for the first time since the death of his dear friend.

Kullmann characteristically stresses that the sequel to these events is provided by the *Aethiopis* (as deduced, again, by combining Proclus' epitome with Pindar *Pythian* VI 28-49: for a detailed treatment of this topic see pages 64-65 below). For there Achilles slays Memnon and thus directly brings about his own death, because Memnon has in his turn killed Achilles' friend and companion Antilochus. Willcock, however, is right to emphasize (1973:8) the further ramifications of the problem.

It is not merely that *Iliad* XXIII also takes up the theme of Antilochus' relationship with Achilles, a feature we have seen to be an integral part of the *Iliad* (page 10 above). Antilochus can hardly be a Homeric invention based on Patroclus if the tradition of his own death is presupposed by *Iliad* VIII. Furthermore, in *Odyssey* xi 465-470, when the ghost of Achilles draws near to Odysseus, it is accompanied by the shades both of Patroclus and of Antilochus. And *Odyssey* xxiv 78–79 explicitly draws attention to Antilochus' status as closest friend to Achilles after Patroclus: "Antilochus, whom you, Achilles, honored above all your friends once Patroclus had died."

Willcock summarizes the complexity of the issues with admirable delicacy (1973:8; cf. Willcock 1983):

> The two stories have evidently come together. Both Patroclus and Antilochus are now buried with Achilles, but Antilochus is treated as secondary. We reach something of an impasse. If we think of Patroclus as the original and Antilochus as the copy, then we are forced to push the Achilles/Patroclus friendship and its fatal consequences back into the tradition, behind Homer; for the poet is evidently aware in *Iliad* VIII and XXIII of the secondary Antilochus story. On the other hand, if we consider Antilochus as the original and Patroclus the copy (as the neo-analysts typically do), then this is not only contrary to the evidence of the *Odyssey*, but we also have to imagine Homer in the Funeral Games preparing the way for his model, creating the conditions for the story of Antilochus. There is one satisfactory explanation. These two stories, which are very like alternative versions of the same story, present in the *Iliad* what would in textual criticism be called a contaminated tradition. Each has affected the other. They co-exist. Neither is by now the absolute model.

The possibility of such reciprocal borrowing or "cross-quotations" was long ago perceived by Gilbert Murray (*The Rise of the Greek Epic* [Oxford 1934] 177–178).

Patroclus (*Iliad*) ∽ Achilles (*Aethiopis*)

In *Iliad* XXIII 192–211 Achilles kindles the pyre on which the body of Patroclus is lying, but it obstinately refuses to burn.[16] The hero has to pray to the Winds Boreas and Zephyrus, promising them abundant sacrifice. Iris "intercepts" the prayer, as it were, and transmits it to the Winds, whom she finds feasting at Zephyrus' palace in Thrace. Having conveyed to them Achilles' prayer and vow, she leaves, and the Winds in turn proceed to Troy and light the pyre.

The passage as a whole has been explicated by Kakridis (1949:76–83). Our business in the present context is with the poet's motive for disrupting his account of Patroclus' funeral with this unexpected digression. "Why do the Winds not come to set [the pyre] burning immediately?" is how Kakridis (80)

---

[16] On this issue see especially Burgess 2001:74–78.

formulates the problem, and his answer involves the hypothesis that in these lines Homer has "imitated either the *Aethiopis* itself or at least its source" (81). For we know of a tradition (preserved in Hesiod *Theogony* 378–380) that Eos is mother of the Winds (Boreas, Zephyrus, and Notus);[17] now suppose that the poet of the *Aethiopis* was likewise aware of this tradition: he will have regarded these Winds as the brothers of Memnon. If, at the funeral of Achilles—which we know this poem to have contained (see page 78 below)—the Winds refused to help ignite the pyre of the hero who had only just killed their brother, the rather baffling scene in the *Iliad* will have had a far more rational model in the *Aethiopis*.

And, indeed, we find an analogous detail in Quintus of Smyrna's account of the funeral of Achilles (III 665–669). There Zeus signifies the death of a supreme hero by sprinkling his pyre with a light shower of ambrosia, and as a mark of honor to Thetis

> Ἑρμείην προέηκεν ἐς Αἴολον, ὄφρα καλέσσῃ
> λαιψηρῶν ἀνέμων ἱερὸν μένος· ἦ γὰρ ἔμελλε
> καίεσθ' Αἰακίδαο νέκυς. τοῦ δ' αἶψα μολόντος
> Αἴολος οὐκ ἀπίθησε.

Is this passage derived from the *Aethiopis*?

It may well be. Few will wish to deny the ingenuity of Kakridis' approach here. He himself candidly confesses (83) the total and unremitting absence of any direct testimony for the hostility which the Winds entertain against Achilles in his reconstruction, and the complete and undeniable lack of any evidence for the Winds' appearance in the *Aethiopis*. But the natural connection between the Dawn and the Winds may perhaps reassure us that Memnon's status as brother of the Winds has more ancient support than the late and fanciful conceit suggested by its occurrence at Callimachus fr. 110.52 (~ Catullus 66.52–53) and Nonnus XXXVII 75. What is particularly impressive is the way in which the interpretation of the Iliadic passage—"as a pale imitation of an older original epic narrative which included both motifs and justified both the refusal of the Winds and the interference of the gods" (83)—mitigates what seems to me to be a genuinely difficult and perplexing feature.

The same cannot, I fear, be said of the other attempts to find in the *Iliad*'s Patroclus an adaptation of the Achilles hypothesized for the *Aethiopis*. When Patroclus forgets the instructions of his friend Achilles and goes so far as to attack the walls of Troy (XVI 698–701) Apollo repels him thrice and at his fourth

---

[17] "Because the wind tends to rise at dawn in Greece" (West *ad* Hesiod *Theogony* 378, quoting Solmsen, *Hesiod and Aeschylus* [*Cornell Studies* 30 (1949)] 57). But this is not always so: cf. C. Neumann and J. Partsch, *Physikalische Geographie von Griechenland* (Breslau 1885) 90–93.

attempt utters the memorable phrase (707) χάζεο, διογενὲς Πατρόκλεες. He had given a similar warning to Diomedes in V 432–442 when that hero rushed at the god himself four times and on the final occasion received the rebuke φράζεο, Τυδεΐδη, καὶ χάζεο (440). Since a clash between Achilles and Apollo would be far more central and integral to the legend of Troy than either of the two parallel clashes already mentioned, it is hardly surprising that Willcock ("Mythological Paradeigma in the *Iliad*," *Classical Quarterly* 14 [1964]: 151n4 = *Oxford Readings in Homer's* Iliad [Oxford 2001] 450n35) came to consider the idea that in the *Aethiopis* Achilles stormed the walls of Troy and was three times pushed back by Apollo. At the fourth time, suggests Willcock, Apollo said χάζεο, Πηλεΐδη or φράζεο, Πηλεΐδη, καὶ χάζεο (the first alternative being, in fact, the admonitory phrase put in Apollo's mouth by Quintus of Smyrna [III 40] shortly before Achilles' death). Achilles, however, ignores the warning (cf. Proclus τρεψάμενος δ' Ἀχιλλεὺς τοὺς Τρῶας καὶ εἰς τὴν πόλιν συνεισπεσών) and proceeds to his own destruction.

Willcock advanced this theory with tact and circumspection ("it is not the purpose of this note to support the theory that the *Aethiopis* provided the themes of the *Iliad* ... but to suggest how composition by theme might involve certain formulas associated with that theme"). Considerably less circumspection had, in fact, already been displayed by Kakridis (83) when he published very similar speculations. But the more cautious approach better fits the numerous uncertainties involved. The application of the warning to Diomedes certainly fulfills an important function within that hero's *aristeia*, whose main theme is the relation of gods to men (see Andersen 1978:47–87, esp. 71–72).

As a sequel to his encounter with this divine warning, Patroclus is killed by a combination of Apollo and two mortals, as he himself protests (XVI 844–854; cf. Thetis' words at XVIII 454–456). Is not Achilles' death in the *Aethiopis* engineered in a remarkably similar way? And does not the motif sit rather awkwardly in the Iliadic context?

To the first question most of us will be disposed to answer "yes." An equally affirmative reply to the second is less readily produced. "Why should the poet make both Patroclus and Achilles die in exactly the same way?" asks Kakridis (88) and does not wait for an answer. But "because he wishes to stress Apollo's persistent hostility to Achilles, and therefore has the god kill Achilles' best friend as well as Achilles himself," would be a perfectly reasonable retort, and, if we chose to, we might embellish it with the cautious qualification that Patroclus does not really die "in *exactly* the same way" as Achilles, for his divine and his mortal assailant act rather more independently of each other than the *Aethiopis* seems to have allowed. Kakridis further asserts the relative incoherence of the motif of divine intervention in the *Iliad*'s case. But when he claims that "Hector did not need the assistance of Apollo in order to kill Patroclus. One feels immediately how incompatible with the noble character of Hector is the interference of the god," we must reply this time that he is laboring under a misconception as to the symbolism and significance of such divine participation in the epics of Homer. Or would he argue that Achilles did not need the assistance of Athena in order to kill Hector at *Iliad* XXII 214–225? More specifically, W. Allan (2005:1–16) has persuasively argued that Homer represents Hector's victory as hollow and "tarnished" (5), and that Euphorbus' role in the killing is necessary for this effect. The idea that the episode is problematic and as such attractively explicable by the hypothesis of Euphorbus' cooperation with Apollo—as derived, a trifle awkwardly, from Paris' cooperation with Apollo in the *Aethiopis*' killing of Achilles—thus becomes less attractive.

The fight over Patroclus' corpse has also been thought to display features that will have had their place in the *Aethiopis*'s treatment of Achilles,[18] but not every detail in the Iliadic scheme need therefore be traced back to this prototype. In particular, Schoeck's suggestion (1961:94)—that the rebuke to Hector from Glaucus at *Iliad* XVII 166–168 ("You did not dare to stand against Ajax") reflects an original rebuke to Paris, the slayer of Achilles—may safely be ignored (cf. Fenik 1968:168, observing the abundance of just such insults in the *Iliad*).

At the start of *Iliad* XVIII Achilles utters a loud cry of grief on learning of Patroclus' death. Thetis hears the cry from the depths of the sea and leads her sister Nereids in a lament (*Iliad* XVIII 50–66). Kullmann (1981:23 = *Homerische Motive*, 82) disputes her right to do so: how can she lament when she does not as yet know *why* Achilles has cried out, and when, even if she did know, she has not the slightest reason to care for Patroclus? The concept is transferred from the *Aethiopis*, he says. This is surely a little insensitive. Since *Iliad* I 417, Thetis has been aware that her son is ἅμα τ' ὠκύμορος καὶ ὀϊζυρὸς περὶ πάντων, and at XVIII 8–11 Achilles recalls how his goddess mother obscurely hinted at Patroclus' death. It is, in addition, more than a little difficult to envisage just how the allegedly "original" scene in the *Aethiopis* operated.[19]

At *Iliad* XXIII 12–18 Thetis arouses in the hearts of the Myrmidons a desire to lament over the corpse of Patroclus. "But the goddess is not at the camp of the Achaeans" (84), protests Kakridis, who remembers that after her delivery of the arms of Achilles she must have returned to her home in the sea. And so again

---

18 Schoeck's more extreme claims (1961:32–37)—to the effect that the *Iliad*'s numerous scenes of fighting over a warrior's corpse and the rarer depictions of battle over a ship or in a god-sent darkness all derive from the *Aethiopis*—are adequately refuted by Fenik (1968:53–54) on the ground that such elements are thematically very common.

19 What hero, dear to Thetis, would cry out in this manner for Achilles? We are in danger of reconstructing an "original" less coherent than the "copy"—quite the wrong relationship for Neoanalysis (see page 6 above)!

the problem's solution must be that Homer has removed XI 13–14 "bodily from an epic description of Achilles' funeral where the presence of the goddess was both necessary and explicit, to use it for Patroclus." Now this is precisely the sort of overrigorous use of realism and inappropriately close scrutiny of what the poet clearly did *not* wish us to scrutinize that Kakridis himself so rightly castigates elsewhere (e.g. 3–4) in his book.

So too *Iliad* XXIII's Funeral Games for Patroclus remind him of the similar events celebrated for Achilles in the *Aethiopis* and lead him, following in the wake of Pestalozzi (1945:33), to pose the inept question (88) "Which is the proto-type and which the imitation?" As we shall soon see (page 78 below), funeral games in memory of a hero are so much the antithesis of rare that there is not the slightest need to narrow down the range of possibilities in this extreme manner. From the picture of the *Aethiopis*'s Achilles as a prototype for the Iliadic Patroclus, our discussion passes seamlessly on to the next topic.

Sarpedon (*Iliad*) ∽ Memnon (*Aethiopis*)

This identification, long a staple feature of Neoanalytical thought, was reas-serted by two American scholars (M. E. Clark and W. D. E. Coulson, "Memnon and Sarpedon," *Museum Helveticum* 35 [1978]: 65–73), whose article handily absolves me of any extensive doxography[20] on the topic. Much of the argument centers around the evidence of art, which I assess separately below (chapter 2).

Clark and Coulson painstakingly establish (1978:65–66) that in this section of the *Iliad* as a whole Sarpedon is an undeveloped and undercharacterized figure, as opposed to the well-developed and fully characterized Patroclus. Sarpedon's main function is to endow Patroclus with a final blaze of glory derived from his killing of a ἡμίθεος—and a son of Zeus at that—just before he dies. All this is very true and very just, but it is hard to see how it advances their case in the slightest. And I find quite incomprehensible their suggestion (67) that XVI 419–477's use of ring composition centering around the death of Glaucus somehow indicates that Sarpedon is the reflection of an older motif such as Memnon.

Let us turn now to the passage where Zeus ponders the saving of his son Sarpedon but is dissuaded by the intervention of Hera (*Iliad* XVI 440–457). This is often taken to be derived from that part of the *Aethiopis* (as reconstructed from the evidence of vase paintings) which shows Eos' endeavors to save her son Memnon (pages 31–32 below): see, for instance, the scholars cited by Clark and Coulson (68n17). On the face of it, these two scenes are more conspicuous

---

[20] Bibliography of earlier discussions in Rzach 1922:2402.24–26. Add to Clark and Coulson's list Howald 1946:69–70 ("Sarpedon ist eine verkleinerte Kopie des Memnon") and now Kullmann 1981:10 = *Homerische Motive*, 71–72.

for their differences than for their similarities. Zeus is a deity quite unlike Eos, and the Iliadic lines have no character equivalent to the *Aethiopis*'s Thetis (Sarpedon's mother, it need hardly be said, is not close to the surface of any reader's mind!). Vase paintings of the Psychostasia usually depict an aloof, impartial, and nonpartisan Zeus: Hermes balances the scales more often than not, and in his capacity as *psychopompos* he may have priority in this role (see page 31 below). Does not Zeus' direct involvement in the present case produce quite a different picture? "Ah," say the Neoanalysts, "that is because the employment of Eos as a model for Zeus' behaviour has distorted his usual role. Zeus has borrowed some of her qualities, just as he has borrowed some of Hermes'." But in the Iliadic scene it is Hera who adopts the aloof nonpartisan stance, and the notion that these qualities have been transferred to her from her husband produces a fantastically complicated sequence of counter- and cross-references and motif-borrowings.

This last consideration puts into perspective the first of several attempts that have been made to convince us that the Iliadic passage under discussion contains various anomalies which may best be explained by the hypothesis of dependence upon the *Aethiopis*'s version. Thus Schadewaldt, followed by Clark and Coulson (1977:68–69), argues that Zeus' role at *Iliad* XVI 431–461 is oddly passive, and his power is diminished in comparison to what we find elsewhere: this whole picture, and especially the idea of Zeus' subservience to the Moirae, (Hera deters him at 441–442 from rescuing a mortal πάλαι πεπρωμένον αἴσηι) stems from the use of the *Aethiopis*'s Eos as a model: her ineffectuality before Fate is intelligible. But all this is unnecessary: if Zeus hesitates before finally deciding on the death of Hector at XXII 168–178, even though that hero is no relative of his, we can hardly be very surprised if he does the same for his own son. And in each case the poet exploits the device to stress an important turning point within the narrative. The relationship between Zeus and the Moirae is, as one might expect, extremely complicated (see, for instance, Dietrich 1965:297), but there is no need to invoke the *Aethiopis* to clarify its labyrinthine twists and turns. Nor, when taken in context, is the notion of Fate the only deterent to Zeus here: as Hera reminds him (446–447),

> φράζεο μή τις ἔπειτα θεῶν ἐθέληισι καὶ ἄλλος
> πέμπειν ὃν φίλον υἱὸν ἀπὸ κρατερῆς ὑσμίνης.

Still on the subject of the Psychostasia, we may cast a brief glance at the reason given for Hector's retreat from the mêlée over Sarpedon's corpse: γνῶ γὰρ Διὸς ἱρὰ τάλαντα (658). In comparison with Homer's usual technique, this seems an uncharacteristically allusive and elliptical reference to Zeus' scales, which are not referred to again in the narrative at large. Have we not here a rudimentary survival from the Psychostasia, what Kullmann (1960:317) calls an "abgekurztes Motiv," explicable only in the light of the *Aethiopis*'s far fuller treatment? The answer "yes" does not force its way quite so readily to my lips as it does for many of the Neoanalysts. Their more generous response may still be right, but there are other ways of explaining this undeniably reticent reference. For the Scales of Zeus (on which see B. C. Dietrich, "The Judgement of Zeus," *Rheinisches Museum* 107 [1964]: 97–125) do in fact appear elsewhere in the *Iliad* (*Iliad* VIII 69–72 and XXII 209–213: Dietrich 1965:294). Why should not the poet be adducing elliptically a feature that figures more fully elsewhere in his own poem? Why bring the *Aethiopis* in at all? And if it must be brought in, why not reverse the relationship usually posited, and suggest (with Dihle [1970:16]) that this epic included a lengthening and expansion of the Διὸς τάλαντα motif by the device of an appeal from the two relevant mothers? The fact is that these holy scales of Zeus, like all the other details mentioned so far, would make sense as vestigial remains of a fuller account in the *Aethiopis*, but do not in themselves constitute independent and adequate proof of the existence of such a relationship.

The same, regrettably, has to be said of the final[21] passage to be considered, the fate of Sarpedon's corpse in XVI 6, which is supposed to reflect the immortality that his mother wins for Memnon in the *Aethiopis*. Again the idea of an interdependence in terms of borrowing seems paradoxical at first sight, for Sarpedon is accorded an actual burial in a real and identifiable place (as Dihle [1970:19] observes), whereas Memnon enjoys eternal life in some wonderland vaguely located at the edge of the world. And the different outlooks on life presupposed by these differing approaches constitute a crucial divergence between Homer and the Epic Cycle (see Griffin 1977:42 = *Oxford Readings in Homer's Iliad*, 372). It is misleading, therefore, for Schadewaldt to talk of Sarpedon's fate as a "reduced" version of Memnon's: misleading and question-begging in the extreme. Once more the exact opposite could easily be argued, and is, for instance, by Rohde (1886.1:85–86 = p. 64 of English translation): "The poet of the *Aethiopis* has tried to outdo the story [of Sarpedon] in the *Iliad* in impressiveness (for it was evidently his model)."

Nor is this basic discrepancy much mitigated by the attendant circumstances with which the central pictures are elaborated. In the *Aethiopis* it is deduced (see below, page 35) that Memnon's body was removed from the battlefield by his mother (appropriately enough). In the *Iliad*, however, it is Apollo

---

[21] Kullmann (1981:10–11, 20 = *Homerische Motive*, 71–73, 79–80), following Reinhardt (1961:357), is especially impressed that in *Iliad* XVI 317–329. Antilochus and his brother Thrasymedes combat two ἑταῖροι of Sarpedon (∞ Memnon). But see Fenik's remarks (quoted above, page 9) on the typicality of the *Iliad*'s (and presumably the *Aethiopis*'s) battles.

who carries out the like task for Sarpedon's corpse (XVI 665–673). He is no close relative of the dead hero.

It would be difficult to devise two more dissimilar scenes—and Apollo's intervention is not totally inexplicable without recourse to the theory that he is a substitute for Eos. On the contrary, there is once again a parallel within the *Iliad* itself for the scene now under discussion. Apollo's anointing of Sarpedon's corpse (670–680) has a very close analogy in the care he takes to protect Hector's body from wear and tear (XXIV 18–21) Apollo's links with Lycia (see Davies and Finglass on Stesichorus fr. 109) will further explain this service rendered to a Lycian hero. Only the motif of Death and Sleep as the conveyors of Sarpedon to Lycia has anything like a strikingly close counterpart in popular reconstructions of the *Aethiopis*, and even there the assumption that Memnon's corpse was escorted by those two daemones is based on evidence that Clark and Coulson themselves admit to be "far less certain."

Hector (*Iliad*) ∾ Memnon (*Aethiopis*)

This equivalence is particularly asserted by Kullman (1981:8–9 = *Homerische Motive*, 69–70). In the *Iliad*, Achilles' killing of Hector sets the seal on his own fate, as his mother foretells. In the *Aethiopis*, Achilles' killing of Memnon sets the seal on his own fate, as his mother (we may plausibly infer [see page 60 below]) foretells; but the difference is that his death follows almost immediately upon the death of Memnon and certainly falls within the scope of the very epic that contains the foretelling.

The motif's impact here is certainly very much more immediate and effective in the form we may infer for the *Aethiopis*. However, one must not underestimate the power the motif possesses in its own right within the *Iliad*: see page 60 below. An agnostic stance over this question is wisely maintained by Willcock (1983:483–484).

We come at last to the final category:

Achilles (*Iliad*) ∾ Achilles (*Aethiopis*)

At the start of *Iliad* XVIII Achilles' extravagant grief over the death of Patroclus is heard by his mother in the depths of the sea as she sits amid her sisters the Nereids (35–38).[22] She leads them in a lament for her son, who she knows will

---

[22] In addition to the instances of this identification cited in the text, note G. M. Sifakis' theory ("*Iliad* 21.114–119 and the Death of Penthesileia," *Bulletin of the Institute of Classical Studies* 23 [1976]: 55–56) that the description of the death of Lycaon in *Iliad* XXI 114–135. is very similar to the depiction of the death of Penthesileia on the famous Munich cup (page 51 below). He deduces that the artifact has been influenced by the *Iliad* or a similar passage in the *Aethiopis*.

shortly die, and then rises up out of the sea and makes her way to Troy. Her sisters follow. When Thetis arrives she takes Achilles' head in her arms and holds it from behind and addresses him ὀξὺ κωκύουσα (71). The significance of this gesture has been brilliantly explained by Kakridis (1949:68–70) in the light of the lamentations for Patroclus and Hector at XXIII 136–137 and XXIV 710–776. In those passages the nearest relative holds the dead man's head, and this practice can be paralleled from vase paintings of the Geometric period (cf. G. Ahlberg, *Prothesis and Ekphora in Greek Geometric Art* [Göteborg 1971]). It is impossible to avoid the conclusion that in this striking scene the prescient Thetis prematurely mourns for Achilles, whose imminent death she can foresee. Is Kakridis's corollary, that the model for the whole picture must be the actual funeral lament over Achilles' corpse as preserved in Proclus' summary of the *Aethiopis*, equally unavoidable? I think not. In the first place Kakridis makes much of the strangely otiose presence of the Nereids in *Iliad* XVIII. They follow their sister out of the sea and all the way to Troy, but they take no part in the encounter between mother and son which then ensues, and indeed their presence jars with the intimacy of that encounter. Perhaps, then, they are there only because the *Aethiopis* represented them as attending the real funeral of Achilles. Perhaps. But we must add that the *Aethiopis* also portrayed the Muses as present at that occasion (see page 73: the fact is stressed by Dihle [1970:21]). Either Homer is following a different source after all or, by restricting the composition of Thetis' escort to her sisters (in whose company she is appropriately discovered in the first place), Homer has adapted the material available to him with considerably more skill than Kakridis allows. Furthermore, the presence of the Nereids is not so superfluous after all if Kakridis' general interpretation of the scene in the *Iliad* is right: "The weeping Nereids fulfil the function of the mourning women at a normal funeral" (Griffin 1980:28).

Already the possibility that the *Aethiopis*'s scene, with the rather anomalous participation of the Muses (see below page 74), represents an attempt to expand and improve on the Iliadic original seems more plausible than the reverse hypothesis outlined above. However, we need not follow that hypothesis through to its logical conclusion here. What we should rather be concerned to stress is that the Iliadic passage makes perfect sense in its own terms without recourse to the hypothesis of a now-lost source in the *Aethiopis*. The *Iliad* is often concerned to look ahead to the future careers of many of its heroes (book XXIII is particularly prone to do this: see the remarks of Willcock [1973:7–9]). Of no character is this more true than Achilles: his death in particular is often foreshadowed to tragic effect (see page 60 below). The present scene takes its place among a number of others within the *Iliad* itself. For the motif of the hero lamented by women while still alive see *Iliad* VI 497–502 on Hector and compare Griffin 1980:28.

We have already anticipated the next item for consideration in our discussion of the last. Several Neoanalysts suppose that the prophecy which Thetis delivers to Achilles in the *Iliad* had an equivalent (far speedier of fulfilment) in the *Aethiopis*. That there are similarities none can deny. But prophecies were so common a feature both in the *Iliad* and in the Epic Cycle that no far-reaching conclusions should be drawn.

The use of αὐτίκα has a poignant and pathetic impact in *Iliad* XVIII 96 (αὐτίκα γάρ τοι ἔπειτα μεθ᾽ Ἕκτορα πότμος ἑτοῖμος) which cannot be properly assessed by a mechanical computation of actual numbers of days remaining to Achilles in the *Iliad* as compared with the *Aethiopis* (see Reinhardt 1961:29–31 and cf. Dihle 1970:22, Allan 2003:14n56 for a fuller account of the passage's effect). And when the parallel between *Aethiopis* and *Iliad* has to be suitably sharpened by the bland adoption of Welcker's hypothesis—taken over with enthusiasm by several scholars (especially Schoeck [1961:8–10])—that Achilles withdrew from the fighting after Thetis' prophecy concerning Memnon (2:174), it is hard not to sympathize with Page's polemic (1963:22–23).

We come now to the death of Achilles. Three brief passages are to be borne in mind. The first is *Iliad* XVI 775–776 (on the death of the charioteer Cebriones in the fighting about the corpse of Patroclus):

> ὃ δ᾽ ἐν στροφάλιγγι κονίης
> κεῖτο μέγας μεγαλωστί, λελασμένος ἱπποσυνάων.

Next is *Iliad* XVIII 26–27 (on Achilles' reaction to the news of the death of Patroclus):

> αὐτὸς δ᾽ ἐν κονίῃσι μέγας μεγαλωστὶ τανυσθεὶς
> κεῖτο.

Last is *Odyssey* xxiv 37–40 (Agamemnon to Achilles on the struggle that arose around the latter's dead body):

> ἀμφὶ δέ σ᾽ ἄλλοι
> κτείνοντο Τρώων καὶ Ἀχαιῶν υἷες ἄριστοι,
> μαρνάμενοι περὶ σεῖο· σὺ δ᾽ ἐν στροφάλιγγι κονίης
> κεῖσο μέγας μεγαλωστί, λελασμένος ἱπποσυνάων.

A comparison of the three suggests to Kakridis (85; cf. Pestalozzi 1945:18, Schadewaldt 1952:168) that the last "was composed for the first time for the death of the great Aeacides, ... and that Homer afterwards took it from there to use it ... once for Cebriones and a second time—slightly altered—for Achilles again, but here a live Achilles." Not every scholar has been convinced. In particular, the use of the phrase λελασμένος ἱπποσυνάων has long been felt to sit oddly upon Achilles (e.g. Page, *The Homeric Odyssey* [Oxford 1955] 103: "to apply such an expression to Achilles would be unthinkable in the older Epic").[23] Dihle (1970:23) has further argued that *Iliad* XVIII displays a correct use of τανυσθείς + adverb whereas the other two passages incorrectly combine κεῖμαι with that adverb. Taking this grammatical observation together with the varying applicability of the formula λελασμένος ἱπποσυνάων, Dihle concludes that, *typologically*, *Iliad* XVIII is the oldest and *Odyssey* xxiv the most recent.[24]

Finally, the last passage that calls for a detailed survey in this section: after killing Hector, Achilles wildly plans to sack Troy but suddenly breaks off upon recalling the death of Patroclus and the need to honor his dead body. Neoanalysts wonder whether this scene does not presuppose a similar prototype in the *Aethiopis*, where Achilles, having killed another distinguished adversary (Memnon), actually did proceed to the sack of Troy, only to meet his own death. If the Iliadic passage were in any way peculiar or anomalous we might be disposed to think along these lines. Some scholars do indeed find it oddly unsatisfactory, and even Lesky objects (1967:75.54): "Liegt doch bei den Schiffen Patroklos unbestattet, an ihn vor allern gilt es zu denken Als ob ein brennendes Troia nicht die grosste aller Ehrungen fur den toten Freund gewesen wäre!"

One's instinctive first reaction is to observe that Achilles can hardly go on to sack Troy in the *Iliad*. A more reasonable second thought is that such a sequel would be considerably inferior to what Homer actually presents us with. Is it not quite in keeping with the presentation of Achilles' character that after the high point of his heroic career, the slaying of the Greeks' greatest enemy, his spirit should soar up in ambitious imaginings and then slump back to earth and mortal thoughts upon remembering his great friend and his own impending death, brought perceptibly nearer by the killing of Hector? Once again, Neoanalysis seems to act as a block to the understanding of a given passage's impact.

---

[23] Kullman (1960:38–39) disagrees, citing Achilles' possession of Xanthus and Balius and Alcaeus fr. 42.14 L–P (of Achilles): ὄλβιον ξάνθαν ἐλάτη[ρα πώλων. The application of so fine a motif as *Iliad* VI 775–776 to the minor character that Cebriones is in our *Iliad* has led scholars who refuse to accept the appropriateness of the expression in Achilles' case to some strange conclusions (e.g. Wilamowitz, *Ilias und Homer*, 142 and n3: Cebriones may have played a larger role in now-lost epics, or the phrase may have been originally invented for Patroclus; W. H. Friedrich [*Verwundung und Tod in der Ilias* (Göttingen 1956) 106] likewise deems the relevant passage a "Fremdkörper"). On Homer's use of pathos for minor characters see Griffin, "Homeric Pathos and Objectivity," *Classical Quarterly* 26 (1976): 161–187 = 1980:103–143.

[24] Similarly Hartmut Erbse, *Beiträge zum Verständnis der Odyssee* (Berlin 1972) 194.

Conclusion

Die Memnonsgeschichte … ist die Erfindung eines Dichters, der bereits
das alte Zornesgedicht kannte, aber *vor* Homer wirkte.

Howald 1946:127

The above examination of the main passages that have been called into play in
investigations of the relationship between the *Iliad* and the *Aethiopis* fully justi-
fies our initial remarks (page 4) about the complexity of the issues involved.

Let us restrict ourselves to similarities best explicable in terms of borrowing.
Sometimes (most notably with the motif of Nestor's rescue [see page 7 above])
the *Iliad* does seem to have drawn on the *Aethiopis*, but elsewhere (e.g. the
conveyance of the corpses of Sarpedon and Memnon [see page 19], the laments
for Patroclus and Achilles [page 12]) the reverse hypothesis seems at least as
plausible. And then there is the question of traditional features. E. R. Dodds
summed up the position with characteristic clarity and economy: "Certain
of the motifs do look as if they had been invented for the Memnon story, but
others, like the Funeral Games and the avenging of a friend, may well have been
drawn by both poets from a dateless traditional stock; and in an oral tradition
it is perfectly possible for two poems which belonged to the repertory of the
same reciters to have influenced each other reciprocally, and to have continued
to influence each other over a long period" (1968:12). Similar views have been
more recently expressed by, for instance, W. Allan: "It is more plausible to think
of a shared epic technique based upon a 'grammar' of typical motifs and situ-
ations, since the pursuit of specific dependence or influence (from Homer to
the cyclic poets or vice versa) is, in the preexisting stage of early Greek epic, a
misleading methodology" (2003:14).

I have left to the end the most significant recent attempt to revise our
understanding of the issue, Martin West's dramatic exposition of "the flaw
in the *Memnonis* theory" ("*Iliad* and *Aethiopis*," *Classical Quarterly* 53 [2003]: 8 =
2012:251). West claims that "the *Iliad* poet knew the story of Achilles' death … but
he did not know the Memnon episode that preceded it in the Epic Cycle," and
that the poet of the *Odyssey* similarly did not know of the Penthesileia episode,
the proof being in each case that neither poet mentions either figure. Further,
the *Nekyia* of the *Odyssey* presents Achilles as present in Hades rather than
on the island of Leuce, whither the *Aethiopis* has Thetis conduct him.

Beginning my retort with the *Odyssey*, I observe that (as West himself
concedes: 10 = 261) Penthesileia's absence may be mere coincidence. Regarding
the *Nekyia*, once the poet had devised the brilliant concept of having his hero

meet his former *hetairoi* in Hades, it would have been inconceivable for him to have omitted the greatest. As for the *Iliad*, it may be precisely because that poem's author borrowed the Memnon motif and transferred it to *Iliad* VIII that he has not (5 = 251) brought Memnon to Troy, "even though he is to play such a major role in the story before Achilles' death. The Lycian contingent is there from the beginning: why not the Aethiopians?" I would reply in contrast that, by reusing the motif in disguised form, the *Iliad* has, as it were, "used it up" and cannot display it or any aspect of it in its original and pristine form. As analogy for such reticence as to "source," I would cite the motif of the Judgment of Paris, which I hope to have shown ("The Judgements of Paris and Solomon," *Classical Quarterly* 33 [2003]: 1–14) the *Iliad* to have similarly adapted and transferred to Hector's visit to Troy in book VI. Having thus been transferred, the motif is not available for appearance in its original shape. It only features, as I would argue, once, very elliptically formulated, near the end of the poem. The parallel with what I would infer for Memnon's absence would actually be even more complete if West is right in his Teubner text to accept deletion of *Iliad* XXIV 29–30.

Let us conclude with the wise words of Burgess: "If we can embrace Neo-Analysis as a 'working hypothesis,' we still need to scrutinize its propositions one by one, rejecting and accepting them as seems appropriate."[25]

---

[25] Jonathan Burgess, "Beyond Neo-Analysis: Problems with the Vengeance Theory," *American Journal of Philology* 128 (1997): 16.

Chapter 2
The *Aethiopis* and Art

U NDER THE RUBRIC OF ART, of course, fall a vast number of books and articles covering a wide range of aspects. From the long list of works that deal with more than one category and are rich in bibliography I select for mention G. E. Lung, *Memnon: Archäologische Studien zur Aithiopis* (diss. Bonn 1912); E. Löwy, "Zur *Aithiopis*," *Neue Jahrbücher für das klassische Altertum, Geschichte und deutsche Literatur und für Pädagogik* 33 (1914): 81–94; I. Mayer-Prokop, *Die gravierten etruskischen Griffspiegel archaischen Stils* (*Mitteilungen des Deutschen Archäologischen Instituts, Römische Abteilung* Suppl. 13 [1967]) 64; and Clark and Coulson 1978. I have found the various remarks of K. Friis Johansen (see his book *The Iliad in Early Greek Art* [Copenhagen 1967] "Index," *s.v.* "Trojan epics") sane and helpful.

Kerostasia/Psychostasia

In *Iliad* VIII 69–74 the battle between Greeks and Trojans is preceded by a scene in which the fates of the two sides are placed in the balance by Zeus.[1] Later (XXII 209–213) the same motif introduces the final encounter between Hector and Achilles:

καὶ τότε δὴ χρύσεια πατὴρ ἐτίταινε τάλαντα,
ἐν δ' ἐτίθει δύο κῆρε τανηλεγέος θανάτοιο
τὴν μὲν Ἀχιλλῆος, τὴν δ' Ἕκτορος ἱπποδάμοιο.
ἕλκε δὲ μέσσα λαβών· ῥέπε δ' Ἕκτορος αἴσιμον ἦμαρ,
ᾤχετο δ' εἰς Ἀΐδαο, λίπεν δέ ἑ Φοῖβος Ἀπόλλων.

---

[1] Scholars have long debated whether there is any significant difference between κῆρες and ψυχαί in this particular context. That there is has been vehemently asserted by, for instance, Wilamowitz (*Glaube der Hellenen* 1.271–272), who points to the obvious fact that Memnon and Achilles are still alive. Recent discussion and bibliography in Dietrich 1965:240–241; M. Hengel, *Achilleus in Jerusalem: Eine spätantike Messingkanne mit Achilleus-Darstellungen aus Jerusalem* (*Sitzungsberichte der Heidelberger Akademie der Wissenschaften Philosophisch-historischen Klasse* [1982]).

We know that Aeschylus composed a now-lost tragedy entitled Ψυχοστασία, which allegedly showed something similar. The testimonia for this drama are collected on pages 374–375 of Radt's edition of Aeschylus' fragments (*TrGF* 3). Note in particular Plutarch *De audiendis poetis* 2 p. 17^A: ἐπὶ τοῦ Διὸς εἰρηκότος Ὁμήρου (*Iliad* XXII 210–213) τραγωιδίαν ὁ Αἰσχύλος ὅλην τῶι μύθωι περιέθηκεν ἐπιγράψας Ψυχοστασίαν καὶ παραστήσας ταῖς πλάστιγξι τοῦ Διὸς ἔνθεν μὲν τὴν Θέτιν, ἔνθεν δὲ τὴν Ἠῶ, δεομένας ὑπὲρ τῶν υἱέων μαχομένων. Σ A *Iliad* VIII 70 (2.313 Erbse): ὁ δὲ Αἰσχύλος ... ἐποίησε τὴν Ψυχοστασίαν, ἐν ἧι ἐστιν ὁ Ζεὺς ἱστὰς ἐν τῶι ζυγῶι τὴν τοῦ Μέμνονος καὶ Ἀχιλλέως ψυχήν (cf. Eustathius 699.31 [2.531 Van der Valk]), Pollux 4.130 (1.240 Bethe): ἀπὸ δὲ τοῦ θεολογείου ὄντος ὑπὲρ τὴν σκηνὴν ἐν ὕψει ἐπιφαίνονται θεοί, ὡς ὁ Ζεὺς καὶ οἱ περὶ αὐτὸν ἐν Ψυχοστασίαι. See Taplin, *The Stagecraft of Aeschylus* (Oxford 1978) 431–432 for some timely skepticism as to just how much of this occurred on stage. Skepticism of a different kind comes from West (2000:245–247 = 237–240), who takes further Taplin's objection to an Aeschylean Zeus on stage and the implied use by Aeschylus of the crane and *theologeion*. He concludes that the author of the relevant play, or at least its prologue and closing scene, with Memnon's body removed by crane, was Aeschylus' son Euphorion, whom West also sees as responsible for the Prometheus trilogy, with its similarly spectacular drama-turgy smacking of a post-Aeschylean date and taste.

Now, we possess numerous vase paintings of a Psychostasia involving Achilles and Memnon. Lung (1912:14–27) was able to list and describe seven of them. Beazley brought the total up to nine (in CB3:44–46), appending of course a limpid synthesis of the evidence. The nine relevant vases are catalogued with bibliography by A. Kossatz-Deissmann in *LIMC* I.1, *s.v.* "Achilleus," 172–175 and VI.1, *s.v.* "Memnon," 453–454. There is a full bibliography of earlier discussions in Beazley (CB3:45n1), to be supplemented by Wüst ("Psychostasie," *RE* 23.2 [1959]: 1439–1458) and Taplin (*Stagecraft of Aeschylus*, 431n2). See further Reichardt 2007:62–70.

In these vase paintings the κῆρες or ψυχαί of the two heroes are repre-sented by a tiny figure in each pan of the scales. In three instances the figures are winged and naked; more often they take the form of armed warriors in an attitude of attack. Thetis and Eos, of course, are regularly present, pleading on behalf of their respective sons. Sometimes the weighing of the souls in heaven is combined with the combat of Achilles and Memnon on earth. Most interesting from our viewpoint, however, is the identity of the deity poising the balance of the scales.[2] In the overwhelming majority of cases it is a bearded Hermes

---

[2] On an Etruscan mirror now in the Vatican (Mus. Greg. Etr. inv. 12257 = Pfister-Roesgen S18 [36–37]). Zeus is vigorously besought by Thetis and Eos while Athena looks on. What he holds in his hands, however, is not a pair of scales but thunderbolts. This detail is plausibly derived from

Figure 1. The "Ricci Hydria" (*detail*). Caeretan black-figure hydria: Zeus weighs the fates of Achilles and Memnon, with Eos and Thetis before him. Attributed to the Ribbon Painter, ca. 520 BCE. Rome, Museo Nazionale Etrusco di Villa Giulia 80983. Photo by Dan Diffendale.

who carries out this task. Zeus is not even present on some vases; on others he is there but sits aside, taking no active role in the proceedings. On only one does he actually hold the scales, displacing Hermes to such an extent that that divinity is no longer present. This is the Ricci hydria in the Villa Giulia (80983: *LIMC* I.1, *s.v.* "Achilleus," no. 797 = VI.1, *s.v.* "Memnon," no. 16: see Figure 1). See Beazley (CB3:44–45), Johansen (*The* Iliad *in Early Greek Art*, 261), and the literature there cited. The work is to be dated ca. 520. As Beazley observes (CB3:45), "The picture is quite different from the others: on the right, Achilles and Memnon are seen fighting; on the left, Zeus is seated, with the goddesses imploring him, Eos kneeling, Thetis standing with outstretched arms."

Now even without the contradiction between the identities of the holder of the scales on almost all of these vases and in Aeschylus' *Psychostasia*, we could say for certain that the artifacts are not inspired by the Aeschylean play, because they predate it. We do not know when Aeschylus' *Psychostasia* was first produced, but the earliest of the vases mentioned above dates from the third quarter of the sixth century, and "some of them are earlier than Aeschylus'

---

the artifact's Etruscan milieu by J. Heurgon, "De la balance aux foudres," in *Mélanges offerts à P. Wuilleumier* (Paris 1980) 193–195.

trilogy can have been and indeed than his first appearance as a writer for the stage" (Beazley, CB3:44). It is not surprising, then, that most scholars have identified the source for these vases with our *Aethiopis*, that the habitually sanguine Coulson and Clark should confidently assert that "these scenes can be *definitely* linked to the *Aethiopis*" (1978:70–71; my italics), and that even the cautious Beazley concludes (CB3:45) that our vases' inspiration "can hardly have been other than" the *Aethiopis*.

It is not surprising: but is it inevitable? The absence of the alleged scene from Proclus' summary of the *Aethiopis* will not sway us in the least towards skepticism (such absences are common). But Dihle (1970:139) mentions Stesichorus as a possible source, and although the conjuring of that particular name would, in any other context, be exceedingly irresponsible and vacuous, in this connection it provides a highly sane and sensible reminder of the hypothetical nature of the theory under discussion and the danger of narrowing down the possibilities at this early stage.

Leaving aside these and other complications, let us now consider the precise repercussions of the thesis that these vase paintings derive from the *Aethiopis*. Did every detail on them occur in that epic? To start with an easy point, no one can seriously maintain that the poem described the κῆρες or ψυχαί of Achilles and Memnon in terms of naked and winged figures or miniature warriors. This is a nice example of the inevitable differences between the poetical and the pictorial modes of representation. An epic poet may casually inform us that

> καὶ τότε δὴ χρύσεια πατὴρ ἐτίταινε τάλαντα
> ἐν δὲ τίθει δύο κῆρε τανηλεγέος θανάτοιο

and leave us to imagine the details. A vase painter who elects to depict the same scene must decide how to present these κῆρε in a form that will be instantly recognized.[3] Likewise the combining of that scene with the actual duel of Achilles and Memnon on earth exemplifies the "telescoping" technique of visual depiction.

As regards the presence of the two mothers at the Psychostasia, most scholars have presumed a straightforward and direct debt to the version of things followed in the *Aethiopis*. Here my own feelings are considerably more complex. Can we be quite sure that the vase painters were incapable of adding

---

[3] As Dietrich has put it (1965:241), "Hermes is imagined as weighing the lots of death of the two heroes which the artist paints in the likeness of the εἴδωλα because he does not know how to draw keres." On winged souls in Greek art, see e.g. O. Waser in Roscher *s.v.* "Psyche" (3.3224); Nilsson *GGR* 1·197–198; J. Bremmer, *The Early Greek Concept of the Soul* (Princeton 1983) 94–95n61. More general discussion of the topic in T. H. Gaster, *Myth, Legend, and Custom in the Old Testament* (New York 1969) 769 and 881.

this detail to a kernel of events basically similar to the narrative we find in *Iliad* XXII 209–213? It may be objected that they seem not to have taken the initiative in the case of the *Iliad* itself, since no extant vase painting depicts the Homeric scene. But there is a speedy reply to this: the mothers of Achilles and Memnon seem to have formed a much more obviously antithetical pairing (their sons were clearly intended as foils to each other [see page 76 below] and so were the mothers). If both were divine and both fetched heavenly armor for their sons from Hephaestus and both won them immortality in the poem we are considering, a vase painter might well choose to symbolize their concern for their offspring by depicting them as spectators of the Psychostasia. This type of combining or telescoping two or more original scenes within one depiction has been mentioned above.

In considering this explanation, one is given pause by a single, solitary factor, the testimony of Plutarch (see page 26 above) concerning Aeschylus' *Psychostasia*. According to Plutarch, we find Aeschylus in this play καταστήσας ταῖς πλάστιγξι τοῦ Διὸς ἔνθεν μὲν τὴν Θέτιν, ἔνθεν δὲ τὴν Ἠῶ, δεομένας ὑπὲρ τῶν υἱέων μαχομένων. If Aeschylus really did portray the scene thus, then it is hard to avoid the conclusion that he borrowed the motif from the *Aethiopis*. Unless he wishes to accept the notion that Aeschylus took the detail over from vase paintings, the cautious scholar will wish to leave open the possibility that some such scene did, after all, occur in the *Aethiopis*.[4] But the cautious scholar will also reflect on the relative insubstantiality of this reconstruction, and the relatively untrustworthy nature of the piece of testimony involved. It is interesting to find Taplin (*Stagecraft of Aeschylus*, 432) concluding (on quite independent grounds) "that not too much should be built on the Plutarch passage. It is unlikely that he had read the play, and he may have misrepresented his source (or his source may itself have been distorted)." In spite of this reservation we will continue to keep an open mind as to the *Aethiopis*. But it is a little ironical that the strongest item of evidence for the two mothers thus featuring in the epic should consist in a literary testimonium referring to quite another poetic composition!

What, finally, of the deity who holds the scales? Beazley (CB3:45) probably expresses the views of most of us when he observes that without the Villa Giulia hydria (page 27 above) we should doubtless take Hermes to have been the presiding god in the *Aethiopis*'s Psychostasia; Aeschylus will then have imported Zeus' occupation of that rôle from the analogous scene in *Iliad* XXII. But in view of the single pre-Aeschylean vase painting that shows Zeus fulfilling this task, "we can no longer say that in the *Aethiopis* it was Hermes who held the

---

[4]   Either hypothesis is formally at odds with Plutarch's implication that Aeschylus' only predecessor in his use of the motif was Homer: cf. Gruppe, *Gr. Myth.* 1.681n6.

balance, and are left to conjecture why the Attic artists placed it in his hand." The seeming absence from any vase painting of the Iliadic weighing of Hector and Achilles' souls would appear to exclude an explanation of Zeus' idiosyncratic presence in terms of contamination between Homer's scene and that of the *Aethiopis*.

How was the scene thus reconstituted for the *Aethiopis* inspired? Analogies between the two Greek scenes of weighing and the judgment of the Dead in ancient Egyptian religion have long been recognized. An Egyptian inspiration behind the Psychostasia has nowhere been more vigorously expounded than by Ernst Wüst in his article "Die Seelenwägung in Ägypten und Griechenland" (*Archiv für Religionswissenschaft* 36 [1939]: 162–171); see too his article *s.v.* "Psychostasie" in *RE* 23.2 (1959): 1441–1458. Add to his bibliography Kullmann's remarks (1960:32–33), which are highly sympathetic to Wüst's views, and the important (and considerably more skeptical) critique by Dietrich ("The Judgement of Zeus," *Rheinisches Museum* 107 [1964]: 97–125; and cf. Dietrich 1965:295–296). Further bibliography on the Egyptian material is to be found in F. Graf, *Eleusis und die orphische Dichtung Athens in vorhellenistischer Zeit* (Berlin 1974) 125n156, and F. E. Brenk, review of Bremmer, *Early Greek Concept of the Soul* (*Gnomon* 56 [1984]: 3n6).[5]

In most versions Anubis places Maat, the goddess of truth and justice (sometimes represented by her ideogram the feather, symbol of truth), in one of the pans of the balance. In the other pan he places the heart of the deceased. Thoth then proceeds to verify the weight, writes down the result on his tablets, and announces it to Osiris, god of the dead, who passes a favorable judgment in cases where the two pans are in perfect equilibrium.

No one will deny the similarities, but Dietrich (1964:111–112 and 114–116) demonstrates important differences too. In particular, the Egyptian weighing of souls was (naturally enough) envisaged as happening after the death of the humans involved: the fates of Hector and Achilles, of Achilles and Memnon, are decided while they still live. And a further point ensues: judgment of the dead seems to many scholars an alien concept that finds no place in Greek religious thinking before the sixth century: see Dodds on Plato *Gorgias* 523^A–524^A (pp. 373–375), Richardson on *Homeric Hymn to Demeter* 367–369 (pp. 270–275). For its role in later Greek literature see A. Setaioli, "L'imagine delle bilance e il giudizio

---

[5]   Add J. Gwyn Griffiths, *The Conflict of Horus and Seth from Egyptian and Classical Sources: A Study in Ancient Mythology* (Liverpool 1960) 74–80, esp. 79–80; C. Seeber, *Untersuchungen zur Darstellung des Totengerichts im Alten Ägypten* (*Münchner Ägyptologische Studien* 35 [1976]); A. J. Spencer, *Death in Ancient Egypt* (Harmondsworth 1982) 144; M. Hengel, *Achilleus in Jerusalem: Eine spätantike Messingkanne mit Achilleus-Darstellungen aus Jerusalem* (*Sitzungsberichte der Heidelberger Akademie der Wissenschaften Philosophisch-historischen Klasse* [1982]) 55–56.

dei morti," *Studi Italiani di Filologia Classica* 44 (1972): 38–54; W. Bühler, *Zenobii Athoi Proverbia 5* (Göttingen 1999) 263–264; J. Gwyn Griffiths, *The Divine Judgement* (Leiden 1990). Nevertheless, I still think it possible that a stray feature of Egyptian religious belief was taken up and adapted by Greek poets for their own ends and to new purposes, or by Greek artists from comparable motives.[6] On the general question of Greek absorption of Egyptian ideas on the judgment of the dead, see F. Graf, *Eleusis und die orphische Dichtung Athens in vorhellenistischer Zeit* (Berlin 1974) 125–126. In such a context the replacement of the Egyptian Anubis and Thoth by their Greek equivalent or near-equivalent would (so Wüst and Kullmann are especially vehement in urging) be a natural step. This particular aspect of Hermes may well be primitive (cf. Nisbet and Hubbard on Horace *Odes* I 10.17, H. Herter, "Hermes: Ursprung und Wesen eines griechischen Gottes," *Rheinisches Museum* 119 [1976]: 215–220, esp. 218n90). The Greeks themselves in later times identified Thoth with Hermes messenger of the gods (cf. Roeder in Roscher *s.v.* "Thoth" (5.861–862); P. Boylan, *Thoth, the Hermes of Egypt* (London 1922); Herter, 210n65) and Anubis with Hermes conductor of souls.

Combat between Achilles and Memnon

A duel between Achilles and Memnon was depicted on the Chest of Cypselus (Pausanias V 19.2: Ἀχιλλεῖ δὲ καὶ Μέμνονι μαχομένοις παρεστήκασιν αἱ μητέρες) and later the Amyclaean throne (Pausanias III 18.12: καὶ Ἀχιλλέως μονομαχιά πρὸς Μέμνονα ἐπείργασται). We have numerous vase paintings of the subject: Lung (1912:28–48) listed sixteen examples, two of which were adequately inscribed. But again the fullest and best account of depictions of Achilles' duel with Memnon is Beazley's (in CB2:13–19), who lists inscribed black-figure vases (15), uninscribed black-figure vases (17), and uninscribed red-figure vases (17–19). There is a selective catalogue with bibliography by A. Kossatz-Deissmann in *LIMC* I.1, *s.v.* "Achilleus," 175–180 and VI.1, *s.v.* "Memnon," 453–455. See further Reichardt 2007:62–70.

---

[6] Boardman reminds me that it is common in Orientalizing or Egyptianizing Greek art for a motif to be borrowed and used for a different purpose, probably without knowledge of what the original model signified (see Boardman, *The Greeks Overseas* [London 1980] 149–157). Compare, for instance, the depiction of Heracles slaying Busiris and his followers on a sixth-century Caeretan hydria now in Vienna (3576: *LIMC s.v.* "Bousiris" C9: illustration in Boardman, *Greeks Overseas*, 150). In the memorable words of Ernst Gombrich (*Art and Illusion: A Study in the Psychology of Pictorial Representation*, 115), "Egyptian renderings of some victorious campaign ... show the gigantic figure of Pharaoh confronting an enemy stronghold with its diminutive defenders begging for mercy. Within the conventions of Egyptian art the difference in scale marks the difference in importance. To the Greek ... the type must have suggested the story of a giant among pigmies. And so he turns the Pharaoh into Heracles wreaking havoc among the puny Egyptians."

It is striking that so many of our specimens resemble the Chest of Cypselus in adding the combatants' mothers to the central μονομαχία. Thetis and Eos (the latter usually winged) stand at either side of their sons, encouraging and supporting their offspring (and in the case of Eos sometimes sustaining him physically and literally as he slumps, wounded at Achilles' hand) on many a vase. When scholars claim that the *Aethiopis* is the source of such depictions—when, for instance, Clark and Coulson write (1978:70) "there can be no doubt ... that these representations have been inspired by the single combat" in that poem—what precisely do they mean? Are we to assume that the epic described each of the relevant goddesses as present on the battlefield?

Anyone making such an assumption is likely to be wrong. In the first place, as Martin Robertson pointed out, "the Grieving Mother is ... a regular type in archaic art" ("*Geryoneis*: Stesichorus and the Vase-Painters," *Classical Quarterly* 19 [1969]: 217–218). See Reichardt 2007:73–77, 83–85. Vase paintings of Heracles' combats with Geryon and Cycnus exemplify this tendency: see Davies and Finglass, *Stesichorus: The Poems* (Cambridge 2015) 233 and 463, where we mention the possibility that the pair of women who adorn several depictions of the fight against Cycnus may have been "transferred" from the duel between Achilles and Memnon. For, as Robertson observes, "the classic example is Eos, always present at the combat of Memnon with Achilles, watching with apprehension as her son rushes in, or mourning already as he is struck down, while Thetis triumphs on the other side" (1969:217).

Nevertheless, and despite the frequency of this motif in ancient art, it might be alleged in reply that most of the instances are descended from Eos and Thetis, and that art took this pair directly from epic. But then there is another consideration to face. While there are numerous vase paintings that show Athena standing behind Heracles during his struggle against Geryon, we are not instantly to assume that this is a literal representation of what happened in Stesichorus' *Geryoneis*: the vase painters may merely be symbolizing her earlier support for Heracles in a council of the gods (see Davies and Finglass, *Stesichorus: The Poems*, 280). So too here: as we have already seen (page 28 above), some vases combine the monomachy of Achilles and Memnon with the Psychostasia, and the presence of the two mothers at the former in depictions restricted to that event may be intended to remind us of or symbolize their previous activity in the latter.

And we must take into account one further factor. A μονομαχία on a vase will occupy little of the available surface and runs the risk of being monotonous. Far better to variegate the scene by symmetrically grouping other figures about the central pair. Again, the most obvious corroboration of this statement

Figure 2. Attic red-figure calyx krater: combat between Achilles and Memnon, with Athena and Eos looking on. Attributed to the Tyszkiewicz Painter, ca. 490–480 BCE. Museum of Fine Arts, Boston, Catharine Page Perkins Fund, 97.368. Photograph © Museum of Fine Arts, Boston.

is provided by illustrations of Heracles' fight with Cycnus (see *Stesichorus: The Poems*, 463 for examples). Here is a further, purely visual, explanation of the appearance of Eos and Thetis in terms of the technique of vase painting.

It will certainly account for the occasional subsidiary figure in the design, as when Athena replaces Thetis on a vase by the Tyszkiewicz Painter (Boston 97.368: *ARV*² 290.1 = *LIMC* I.1, *s.v.* "Achilleus," no. 833 [ca. 480]: see Figure 2) and on one or two other vases besides (e.g. Louvre G342: *ARV*² 590.12 = *LIMC* I.1, *s.v.* "Achilleus," no. 839 = VI.1, *s.v.* "Memnon," no. 46 [ca. 460]). Now it is perfectly true that the *Aethiopis*'s Athena could quite easily have helped Achilles against Memnon just as she helped him against Hector in *Iliad* XXII 214–231, but the vases are not necessarily evidence that she did.[7] Likewise with such supernumeraries as Memnon's charioteer (labeled) on an Aeolian black-figure vase in Izmir (*LIMC* VI.1, *s.v.* "Achilleus," no. 810 = VI.1, *s.v.* "Memnon," no. 28) or Automedon (Florence 4210: *LIMC* I.1, *s.v.* "Achilleus," no. 809 = VI.1, *s.v.* "Memnon," no. 35 [ca. 540]); on the use of chariots as space-fillers in several vase paintings of the fight between Heracles and Cycnus, see Davies and Finglass, *Stesichorus: The Poems*, 463.

An incidental figure only once creates serious problems from our point of view. The vase by the Tyszkiewicz Painter mentioned above has a dead warrior lying between the two principal combatants, and he is labeled "Melanippus" rather than the usual "Antilochus." Who is he? Does he derive from the *Aethiopis*? Robert (*Scenen der Ilias und Aithiopis auf einer Vase der Sammlung des Grafen Michael Tyskiewicz* [Hallisches Winckelmannsprogramm 15 (1891)] 3) took him to be a Trojan whom Memnon encountered in the fray. Lung (1912:46–48), noting that Melanippus' corpse faces towards Achilles, deduced that he is meant to be interpreted as a Greek: the rule thus implied is usually observed, but Beazley (CB2:14–15) is able to cite five exceptions, and even if we set aside these significant exceptions, we are not obliged to accept as corollary Lung's conclusion that the name is a slip for Antilochus. Clearly there are other possibilities. For instance, there is Beazley's suggestion (CB2:15) that in Melanippus "the artist has selected a more obscure figure from Memnon's *aristeia*, which must have included several victims beside Antilochus."

The majority of vases show Achilles confronting Memnon with his spear. This is the weapon he uses to kill that hero in Pindar *Nemean* VI 52–53 (φαεννᾶς υἱὸν εὖτ᾽ ἐνάριξεν Ἀόος ἀκμᾶι ἔγχεος) and Philostratus *Imagines* I 7.1 (βέβληται δὲ κατὰ τὸ στέρνον ἐμοὶ δοκεῖν ὑπὸ τῆς μελίας) and presumably in the *Aethiopis*.[8]

Eos and the Corpse of Memnon

Pollux 4.130, in a list of pieces of theatrical equipment, mentions the use of the θεολογεῖον in Aeschylus' *Psychostasia* (see page 26 above), and then continues (presumably speaking of the same play): ἡ δὲ γέρανος μηχάνημά ἐστιν ἐκ μετεώρου καταφερόμενον ἐφ᾽ ἁρπαγῆι σώματος, ὧι κέχρηται Ἡὼς ἁρπάζουσα τὸ σῶμα τὸ Μέμνονος. Whether this tragedy really did display Eos "flying through

---

[7] Athena's presence between two fighting warriors is anyway a common motif in vase paintings from the mid-sixth century onwards. See the examples and discussion offered by Johansen (*The Iliad in Early Greek Art*, 262–263), especially his concluding generalization that "Athena between two struggling heroes is a favourite pattern, which in different variations might be used in many contexts."

[8] On the incompatible scheme in Quintus Smyrnaeus 2.445–446 see Vian *ad loc.* (i.73n1).

the air at the end of a rope suspended from a crane," as Page colorfully put it (*Aeschylus. Agamemnon* [Oxford 1957] xxxi), need not concern us here (for some skepticism see Taplin, *The Stagecraft of Aeschylus*, 432–433). What we are interested in is a number of vase paintings, pre-Aeschylean[9] in date, which depict Eos variously mourning, anointing, or raising the body of her dead son (which is often shown as still bleeding). She is generally winged, and on some vases she is to be conceived of as flying upwards with her son, so that Ἠὼς ἁρπάζουσα τὸ σῶμα τὸ Μέμνονος would be an accurate description of the scene.

Scholars have generally concluded that the *Aethiopis* portrayed Eos as removing her son's corpse from battle.[10] In that poem Eos figured as a parallel in many respects to Thetis (on which see page 18 above), and since Proclus' summary mentions ἐκ τῆς πυρᾶς ἡ Θέτις ἀναρπάσασα τὸν παῖδα one would not be unduly surprised to find that Eos did something similar before gaining immortality for her son.[11] West (2013:148–149) rightly questions what sort of immortality Memnon could have had: the need to complete the parallel was the most important factor.

The relevant vases were listed by Lung (1912:51–53). A fuller list, description, and bibliography, together with illustrations of many of the vases, were provided by A. Minto, "Lamine di bronzo figurate a sbalzo di arte paleoetrusca in stile protoionico," *Monumenti Antichi* 28 (1922): 268–288. Still more up-to-date are the lists and information produced by Mayer-Procop (1967:65); cf. von Bothmer, "Notes on Makron," in *The Eye of Greece: Studies in the Art of Athens* (Martin Robertson Festschrift [Cambridge 1982]) 33, 41; Reichardt 2007:77–81. Two black-figure and three red-figure Attic vases, all roughly contemporaneous, depict the scene. Memnon and Eos are only labeled as such on two vases, but this is enough to allow secure identification of the scene on the remainder. The episode also appears on Etruscan mirrors: see the specimen now in Copenhagen (National

---

[9] In the sense indicated page 28 above.

[10] Perhaps after first lamenting over him (Fenik, *Iliad X and the Rhesus: The Myth* [Collection Latomus 73 (1964)] 32n4). On the meaning of the similar phrase ἡ Θέτις ἀναρπάσασα τὸν παῖδα see page 76 below.

[11] Antiquity represented Eos as generally addicted to the snatching up and carrying off of young men (usually from erotic motives, of course); cf. Σ *Odyssey* v 1 (on the story of Tithonus): ἡ δὲ θεραπεία τοῦ μύθου ὅτι τοὺς ἔτι νέους ὄντας καὶ ἀφνιδίως ἀποθνήισκοντας ἔλεγον ἁρπάζεσθαι παρὰ τῆς Ἠοῦς; ps.-Dionysius of Halicarnassus, *Art of Rhetoric* VI 5 (2.282.6–9 Usener–Radermacher): εἰ μὲν νέος ὢν τοῦτο πάθοι ὅτι θεοφιλής· τοὺς γὰρ τοιούτους φιλοῦσιν οἱ θεοί. καὶ ὅτι καὶ τῶν παλαιῶν πολλοὺς ἀνήρπασαν, οἷον τὸν Γανυμήδην, τὸν Τιθωνόν, τὸν Ἀχιλλέα; cf. Horace *Odes* I 28.8 and Nisbet-Hubbard *ad loc.*, and West on Hesiod *Theogony* 986–991. Also D. D. Boedeker, *Aphrodite's Entry into Greek Epic* (*Mnemosyne* Suppl. 31 [1974]) 66–68 and "Index I" (93) *s.v.* "Dawngoddess ... erotic role of"; S. Kaempf-Dimitriadou, *Die Liebe der Götter in der Attischen Kunst des 5 Jahrhunderts v. Chr.* (Basel 1979) 16–21 and P. Bloch, *LIMC* III.1 (1986), *s.v.* "Verfolgung eines Geliebten," 759–779 (artistic evidence).

Figure 3. Etruscan bronze mirror: Eos with the corpse of Memnon.
From Piansano, ca. 470–450 BCE. Copenhagen, National Museum of
Denmark 3403. Drawing courtesy of the National Museum of Denmark.

Museum inv. 3403: Mayer-Prokop 1967:64–67 = Pfister-Roesgen S24 [43–44]; *LIMC*
VI.1, *s.v.* "Memnon," no. 84: see Figure 3) and that in Berlin–Charlottenburg
(Staatliche Museen Fr. 28 = Pfister-Roesgen S14 [33–34]; *LIMC* VI.1, no. 82).

This seems the simplest and least problematic correlation between the
evidence of art and our epic. Ironic again, then, that the episode presumably
reflected is not directly attested by any literary source.

Memnon (?) Transported by Sleep and Death

On this group of vases see most recently von Bothmer 1981:72–80 and in *LIMC* VII,
(1994), *s.v.* "Sarpedon," 697. Here even the usually sanguine Clark and Coulson
confess (1978:71) that "the identification of the scene as stemming from the
Aethiopis is far less certain." Lung (1912) cited four vases:

- Black-figure neck-amphora by the Diosphos Painter (Louvre F388: *LIMC*
  VII.1, no. 7).

- Black-figure cup (the relevant scene is repeated on both sides) in the manner of the Haemon Painter (Athens National Museum [ANM] 505: *ABV* 564.580 .
- Red-figure cup by the Nicosthenes Painter (British Museum [BM] E12: *ARV*² 126.24 = *LIMC* VII, no. 5).
- Red-figure calyx-krater by the Eucharides Painter (Louvre G153: *ARV*² 227.12 = *LIMC* VII, no. 6).

Despite individual differences (presently to be detailed) it may be said that each of these vases shows two winged beings transporting a corpse. For a useful historical survey of scholarly interpretations of these artifacts see von Bothmer 1981:72–73 and 76–77 and in *LIMC* VII.1, *s.v.* "Sarpedon," 698–700. Robert (*Thanatos* [39. *Programm zum Winckelmansfeste* (Berlin 1879)] 4–8) alone of earlier scholars detected Sarpedon's body, while Löwy in particular ("Zur *Aithiopis*," 81–83), closely followed by Mayer-Prokop (1967:65–66), argued strongly that we have here depictions of the brothers Ὕπνος and Θάνατος carrying Memnon, on his mother Eos' behalf, to the regions where she is especially at home, the boundaries of the Earth and the shores of Oceanus: here he will dwell immortal forever (cf. *Homeric Hymn to Aphrodite* 227, where Tithonus lives with Eos, and Pindar *Olympian* II 83 [Memnon among the heroes in the Islands of the Blessed]).

On this particular area of inquiry, perhaps the most useful introduction is the luculent summary by Lesky in *RE s.v.* "Thanatos" (5ᴬ [1934]) 1250–1251 and 1260. See too K. Heinemann, *Thanatos in Poesie und Kunst der Griechen* (diss. Munich 1913) 56–68 (on "Thanatos und Hypnos auf den mythologischen Vasenbildern"); Johansen, *The* Iliad *in Early Greek Art*, 255–256; von Bothmer 1981, which provides illustrations of the relevant works (plates 74–87); and *LIMC* VII, as cited.

Now for a more detailed account of these artifacts. Louvre F388 shows an unbearded corpse held in the arms of Sleep and Death. Above the corpse flies its *ker*, which is depicted as armed and winged.[12] In view of our above discussion of the numerous motifs shared by the stories of Memnon and Sarpedon (page 16), we at once ask, "Why should not the corpse belong to the latter?" The depiction "is best viewed as derived from the *Aethiopis*," according to Clark and Coulson (1978:72) because there is "no mention of an εἴδωλον in the rather detailed and highly descriptive passage in" *Iliad* XVI 631–635 on the death of Sarpedon. But

---

[12] A very similar composition on a neck-amphora by the same painter (New York inv. 56.171.25) shows the corpse bearded and the two carriers sans wings. "Hence it is doubtful whether they are meant to be Hypnos and Thanatos" (Johansen, *The* Iliad *in Early Greek Art*, 255). It is also doubtful whether the corpse is Memnon's (it is Sarpedon's, according to Dietrich von Bothmer, "Greek Vases from the Hearst Collection," *Bulletin of the Metropolitan Museum of Art* 15 [1957]: 172 and in *LIMC* VII.1, no. 8 [p. 697]).

Figure 4. Attic red-figure cup: Hypnos and Thanatos with the body of Sarpedon, attended by two female figures. Attributed to the Nikosthenes Painter,
ca. 510–500 BCE. London, British Museum 1841,0301.22 (Vase E12).
Photograph © British Museum.

this is precisely the sort of detail an artist would add to clarify matters (see
above on the Psychostasia [page 28]).

ANM 505 contains a central group consisting of a bearded corpse again
carried in the arms of Sleep and Death, and tended by a winged female. To the
right of this group stands a bearded male figure wearing high boots and carrying
a *petasos*. Several scholars have claimed him as Hermes Psychopompus (e.g.
Robert, *Thanatos*, 18; Clark and Coulson 1978:71). To the left, a young woman
and a young man, identified as Memnon's wife and brother by Robert (17–18).
The vase's status as a representation of Death and Sleep translating the corpse
of Memnon in the presence of his mother is accepted by, for instance, Beazley
and von Bothmer. But we cannot decide the issue in isolation from the other
alleged instances of the story.

British Museum E12 (see Figure 4) likewise displays a central group, similar
to that of ANM 505. To the right of this we find a female figure with her right arm
stretched towards the corpse. To the left a female figure bearing a caduceus—
"she can be identified as Iris, who, as the messenger of the gods, has called Sleep
and Death to the place where Eos has washed and annointed Memnon's body"
(so Clark and Coulson [1978:72], who, not surprisingly, choose to interpret the
other female form as the grief-stricken Eos). The corpse has been identified with
Sarpedon and the mourning woman on the right consequently as his mother,
Europa, by scholars of the calibre of Beazley, Robertson (1969:217–218), and
von Bothmer (first in "Greek Vase Painting," *Bulletin of the Metropolitan Museum
of Art* 31 [1972]: 34–35, and then in 1981:71–73; and *LIMC* VII) as earlier by e.g.
Wilamowitz (*Ilias und Homer*, 135 and 141) or Schmid, *GGL* 1.1.211n4. According to

Clark and Coulson, "such an identification ... is difficult to substantiate" (1978:72) because, instead of Apollo and Zeus (whom the Iliadic narrative would lead us to expect), we see two female figures, neither of whom Homer finds cause to mention. But again, the presence of these figures has an artistic rather than a literary motive, one that is amply explained by Robertson's reminder (cited page 32 above) that "the Grieving Mother ... is a regular type in archaic art."

Louvre G153, as Clark and Coulson allow, is in its "origin ... more ambiguous." Indeed, it simply depicts a bearded corpse held in the arms of Sleep and Death, and that corpse has been presumed to be Sarpedon by, for instance, Beazley and von Bothmer.

It is time to stress the very real danger of circular argument. The American scholars' interpretation of this last scene as the transportation of Memnon's body rests merely on their assumption of "the popularity of the Memnon story as an inspiration for artistic representation" (Clark and Coulson 1978:72). Johansen too—as part of a general defense of all the vases' reference to Memnon rather than Sarpedon—asserts that "whereas Memnon is an extremely popular figure in archaic Greek art, Sarpedon is depicted very rarely there" (*The* Iliad *in Early Greek Art,* 256). But by the start of the twenty-first century it could be claimed that, on the contrary, "the death of Sarpedon is by far the more popular picture," with "only one vase certainly depicting Memnon carried by" Hypnos and Thanatos: J. H. Oakley, "A New Black-Figure Sarpedon," in *Essays in Honor of D. von Bothmer* I, ed. A. J. Clark and J. Gaunt (Amsterdam 2002), 246, noting ten Attic vases and two South Italian that depict the former theme, and adding another on an olpe in Sydney (cf. J. R. Mertens, "Laodamas and Hippolytus," in the same volume, 211–212).

An element of complexity is introduced by Louvre G153's subsidiary figures: a bearded Hermes with winged petasos and wand; and on either flank of the central scene a warrior, one labeled Laodamas and the other Hippolytus.[13] Clark and Coulson stubbornly maintain that Hermes has replaced the *Iliad*'s Apollo because of contamination with the story of Memnon (for the alleged rôle of Hermes Psychopompus in which see page 29 above). That story's popularity in art of the last decade of the sixth century would thus be strengthened still further by the apparent motif-transference. But in fact, the presence of Hermes Psychopompus is an obvious adjunct to the brothers Sleep and Death, and requires no such hypothesis of contamination to explain it (cf. von Bothmer 1981:69). The American scholars would reverse Dietrich von Bothmer's original assumption (*Bulletin of*

---

[13] They are taken by von Bothmer ("Der Euphronioskrater in New York," *Archäologischer Anzeiger* 80 [1976]: 485–512) to be Lycian and Trojan names, and to symbolize the Trojan battlefield from which Sarpedon is being spirited away (compare his remarks 1981:69–70). Clark and Coulson (1978:72) prefer to suppose that they represent those Trojans and their allies who gave Sarpedon his last rites.

the *Metropolitan Museum of Art* 31 [1972]: 34–35, elaborated 1981:71–72) to the effect that the portrayal of Sleep and Death on BM E12 above is adopted from Euphronius' krater. But it is time to face the fact (however hard and unpalatable) that the only example of a labeled corpse transported by Sleep and Death gives that corpse's identity as *Sarpedon*.

Conversely (and equally awkward for the theory under discussion), when on one vase the corpse can safely be interpreted as Memnon's (a late black-figure lekythos: *LIMC* VI.1, *s.v.* "Memnon," no. 61) it is because that corpse is being conveyed by two Ethiopians and not by a winged pair of carriers. Even if the earlier ANM 505 does relate to Memnon's conveyance by the same pair, we may choose to argue (with von Bothmer [1981:78]) that it represents a rare "conflation of the traditional scene of Sleep and Death with the body of Sarpedon, and those pictures that show Eos mourning her dead son."

This brings us to the strongest objection to the theory under discussion: the impropriety of Hypnos and Thanatos as the conveyors of Memnon's corpse.[14] One is familiar with the frequent allusions in ancient literature to the similarity of the two states personified by the two brothers (see e.g. O. Waser in Roscher *s.v.* "Thanatos" (5.482–518); Nisbet and Hubbard on Horace *Odes* 1.24.5). Since Memnon is being transported to immortality, it is hard to see why Thanatos should have a hand in the proceedings at all; and since Hypnos can only be present as a companion for his brother, the twins do indeed seem totally and grotesquely out of place (cf. Lesky 1934:1249.48–60). Not so in the *Iliad*, where their presence has been adequately explained by, e.g. Rohde, 1886.1:86n1 = 84n28 (Engl. transl.); cf. Lesky 1934:1249.57–59: "Auf Thanatos aber kommt es in erster Linie an, denn ihm gesellt sich der Schlaf als sein Bruder bei und nicht umgekehrt."

It is not as if several far more appropriate candidates do not offer themselves for the task. If the evidence of vases (page 35 above) indicates that Eos snatched her son's corpse from the battlefield, why should she not transport him personally to the region at the end of the world (see page 18 above) where she is so much at home? The motif underlying the whole myth (page 35 above) and the parallel between Eos and Thetis (page 35 above) require that the goddess herself

---

[14] There is no evidence for Gruppe's guess (*Gr. Myth.* 1.682n1, followed by Kullman [1960:36n1]) that the *Aethiopis* made Eos daughter of Nyx (like Quintus Smyrnaeus II 626) and therefore sister of Thanatos and Hypnos (offspring of Nyx according to Hesiod *Theogony* 212, which, however, has quite a different parentage for Eos [371–373]). Perhaps the bravest defense is Rzach's (2402.4–8): "In sinnvoller Darstellung gilt der eine als Symbol des Todes, dem Memnon eben verfiel, während der andere kunden soll, dass der Held nur schlafe, um zu neuem ewigen Leben zu erwachen" (similarly Pestalozzi 1945:13–14). Rohde (1886.1:86n1 = 84n28 [Engl. transl.]) supposed the frequent equating of sleep and death in funerary epigrams (cf. R. A. Lattimore, *Themes in Greek and Latin Epitaphs* [Urbana 1962] 164) to explain the presence of the brothers on the vases (though not in Homer, whose use of them he supposed [see page 18] to predate the *Aethiopis*'s employment of the motif).

should carry the young man to her home. In the words of Wilamowitz, such a hypothesis is easier than the assumption that "erst Aischylos die Eos selbst ihren Sohn aus dem Schlachtfelde tragen liess. Eos hat ja auch den Tithonos und den Kephalos selbst entführt: sie bedarf also keiner anderen Hilfe" (*Ilias und Homer*, 141).

Supposing that, for some reason, Eos *is* unable to convey her own son to everlasting bliss: there are more suitable delegates for her to approach than Sleep and Death. "One is familiar with passages where a dead person is said to be wafted away by the winds" (Nisbet and Hubbard, *A Commentary on Horace Odes Book I*, 327, referring us to their note on 1.2.48). In fact this is precisely how the operation is performed in Quintus Smyrnaeus II 550–555 (cited, for instance, by Rohde, 1886.1:86.1 = 84n28 [Engl. transl.]):

θοοὶ δ' ἅμα πάντες Ἀῆται
μητρὸς ἐφημοσύνῃσι μιῇ φορεόντο κελεύθωι
ἐς πεδίον Πριάμοιο καὶ ἀμφεχέαντο θανόντι·
οἵ καὶ ἀνηρείψαντο θοῶς Ἠοίον υἶα
καὶ ἑ φέρον πολιοῖο δι' ἠέρος ἄχνυτο δέ σφι
θυμὸς ἀδελφεοῖο δεδουπότος κτλ.

The last words cited remind us of Kakridis's theory (page 13 above) that the *Aethiopis* portrayed the Winds as unwilling to help kindle their brother's pyre. I am reluctant to heap hypothesis upon hypothesis by framing the rhetorical demand "Who more appropriate to convey Memnon to immortality?"[15] My concern is rather to stress the gulf that separates all theories concerning the role of Sleep and Death in our epic from any semblance of certainty.

Suppose we were miraculously to learn that the vases in question do depict Thanatos and Hypnos transporting Memnon's corpse, and do draw upon the *Aethiopis* as their source. Even then it would by no means follow automatically and inevitably that Thanatos and Hypnos fulfilled that role in that epic. The possibility that the relevant vase painters[16] themselves borrowed those

---

[15] It has indeed been suggested that the two winged figures on the vases considered above should be identified as wind gods. For bibliography and arguments against see O. Waser in Roscher *s.v.* "Thanatos" (5.484.40–59). On winged wind gods in general see Pearson on Sophocles *TrGF* 4 F23.3 (Radt) (1.19); H. Lloyd-Jones, "Notes on Sophocles' *Antigone*," *Classical Quarterly* 7 (1957): 25 = *Academic Papers* [I], 383–384; K. Neuser, *Anemoi: Studien zur Darstellung der Winde und Windgottheiten in der Antike* (Rome 1982).

[16] Memnon's transportation by Death and Sleep has also been detected on an Etruscan mirror that is no longer extant (cf. Mayer-Prokop 1967:125–127 [with plate 56 = Pfister-Roesgen]) and two Etruscan gems from the first half of the fifth century (New York 42.11.28; Boston, Lewis House Collection, where, however, as von Bothmer observes [1981:78], it "cannot be excluded that the winged figures are mere daemons of death of which the world of Etruria is full, and the dead an ordinary mortal").

Figure 5. Megarian terracotta relief bowl: series of "Homeric" scenes, including Penthesileia before Priam. Once Berlin, Staatliche Museen 3161h (now lost). Drawing after C. Robert, *Homerische Becher* (Berlin 1890), p. 26, fig. D.

two daemons from *Iliad* XVI 676–683 and transferred them to Memnon (so, for instance, Wilamowitz [*Ilias und Homer*] or Lesky 1934:1250.13; cf. von Bothmer 1981:77) cannot be excluded.

Several "Homeric cups" (listed most recently by U. Sinn, *Die Homerischen Becher* [Berlin 1979] 92–93 [cf. plates 12–14] and *LIMC* VII.1, *s.v.* "Penthesileia," nos. 3a and 3b) provocatively juxtapose a scene we know to have occurred near the end of the *Iliad* with two scenes that in all probability occurred near the start of the *Aethiopis*. A summary of the contents of the famous specimen once in Berlin (Staatliche Museen [previously Königliches Antiquarium] inv. 3161h: MB23 = *LIMC* VII.1, *s.v.* "Penthesileia," nos. 3a = *s.v.* "Priamos," no. 71a: see Figure 5)—of which Robert (*Homerische Becher* [Berlin 1890] 25–28) provided a detailed description and discussion—may serve for the rest too. In the first scene, a kneeling Priam beseeches a standing Achilles within his tent (here, as everywhere else on this cup, the relevant figures are clearly identified with labels). In the next scene the same Priam, this time standing at the left rather than kneeling to the right, faces and clasps the hand of the Amazon Penthesileia.

As Weitzmann (*Ancient Book Illumination*, 44) says of another example of this same gesture in plastic art, Priam and the Amazon "shake hands, not as a sign of mere greeting but of making an oath which seals their alliance"; cf. S. D. Olsen on Aristophanes *Acharnians* lines 307–308. Between them stands a στήλη labeled as the τάφος Ἕκτορος. Penthesileia's eagerness to be off to the fray seems to be indicated not merely by the double-headed axe in her other hand but by the stance of her whole body, especially her legs. In the third scene her wish has been fulfilled, and, still standing to the right, she brandishes her axe and holds her shield against an Achilles who is naked but for boots, plumed helmet, long spear, and circular shield, the latter two of which are poised for combat with her. Weitzmann (*Ancient Book Illumination*, 44) boldly opined that "if the several lines of rubbed writing above the handshake of Priam and Penthesileia in front of Hector's tomb could be read, they most likely would turn out to be from the *Aethiopis*."[17]

One obviously sympathizes with the comparison Robert draws between this cup and the notorious "alternative ending" to the *Iliad* (28). But the analogy is by no means exact (the two lines in question juxtapose Hector's funeral and the Amazon's arrival), and an impartial examination of the passage reveals that these hexameters have no claim to derive from the *Aethiopis* (let alone from that poem's opening): see pages 90–94 below.

Weitzmann (*Ancient Book Illumination*, 46) comes to the conclusion "that two different recensions are involved: one represented by the Megarian bowl which depicts Penthesileia without the horse but with the tomb of Hector, and the other by the Iliac tablet, the sarcophagus lid, and the Pompeian fresco, all of which show Penthesileia with her horse but without Hector's tomb."[18] However, the point to stress here is that each version is marked out by the balance and symmetry of its design as artistic rather than literary in origin. Thus it would be rash, for instance, to excogitate, on this evidence alone, an epic scene in which Priam greeted Penthesileia at the tomb of his son: the function of the tomb on the depictions considered above is to remind us that the Amazon queen is succeeding Hector as the mainstay of Troy. It may even be rash to deduce (with Robert, *Heldensage* 2.1177) that that epic had Penthesileia arrive on the very day of Hector's obsequies; similarly West 2013:138.

In view of all this it is hard to see why Weitzmann should so automatically presume (*Ancient Book Illumination*, 45) that the scenes which accompany Penthesileia's pledge to Priam on the sarcophagus lid derive from the *Aethiopis* and thus constitute "a representation of a text passage no longer in existence." These scenes are, respectively, to the left of Penthesileia a group of women in mourning: they include Andromache holding Astyanax in her lap while Hecuba approaches her from behind; and to the right the consoling of Andromache— who holds the ashes of her husband in her lap—by a Paris clad in a Phrygian cap; and a number of Amazons arming for battle. Again the subject matter is the sort that would instinctively occur to any artist.

---

[17] Far more cautious an appraisal from Robert: "zu entziffern habe ich nichts vermocht, kann daher auch nicht entscheiden, ob es Verse waren ... oder eine allgemeine Bezeichnung der dargestellten Scene" (*Homerische Becher* 27–28).

[18] The sarcophagus lid is *LIMC* VII.1, *s.v.* "Penthesileia" B5, and the other artifact is B7.

Chapter 3

Commentary on Proclus'
Summary of the *Aethiopis*

THE QUESTION OF A DATING OF THE COMPOSITION relative to the *Iliad* has been considered above (pages 3–24), where it was seen to be an exceedingly complex issue. As for an *absolute* dating, the epic has a traditional author (Arctinus) who in turn is assigned a traditional *floruit*. The inadequacy of such traditions is now generally recognized.

We might stand in a stronger position could we accept the argument of F. Heichelheim ("The Historical Date for the Final Memnon Myth," *Rheinisches Museum für Philologie* 100 [1957]: 259–263), which claims to present a *terminus post quem* of between 663 and 656,[1] inasmuch as it is there stated that the Memnon myth reached its complete and final version at such a date. The alleged justification for this is that Ctesias (*FGrHist* 688 F1) represents the Assyrian king Tentamus as sending an Aethiopian Memnon to help a Priam who is depicted as an Assyrian vassal, and 663–656 was a period when Assyria did, as a matter of historical fact, control Aethiopia. As implied above, it is no obstacle to this hypothesis to object that Arctinus' *floruit* is positioned a whole century earlier than this. But as R. Drews has pointed out ("Aethiopian Memnon: African or Asiatic?," *Rheinisches Museum für Philologie* 112 [1969]: 191–192), the Memnon of myth is an Asiatic Oriental, the Eastern son of Dawn, unconnected with the real world's African Ethiopia, spreading awareness of which among Greek authors did not instantaneously lead to the enrollment of the legendary Memnon among the Africans: on the contrary, Aeschylus, for instance, made him a Cissian; only Hellenistic writers portray him as African.

On the possible relevance of Milesian colonization of the Black Sea area for the dating of our epic see page 76 below.

---

[1] This happens to coincide with the dating arrived at by West (2013:135–137) on independent grounds relating to his theory of an *Amazonis* and a *Memnonis* underlying the *Aethiopis*. For some negative comments see pages 23–24 above.

ἐπιβάλλει δὲ τοῖς προειρημένοις {ἐν τῆι πρὸ ταύτης βίβλωι} Ἰλιὰς Ὁμήρου
Following the aforementioned poems comes Homer's Iliad.

For the meaning of the verb here and the consequences that follow from it, see my forthcoming commentary on the *Cypria*.

μεθ᾽ ἥν ἐστιν Αἰθιοπίδος πέντε βιβλία
After which come the Aethiopis's five books.

For this type of phraseology used of one work appended to another cf. West's commentary on Hesiod's *Theogony*, p. 402. For the exact translation of the reference to the number of books see Burgess 2001:30.

Penthesileia

Ἀμαζὼν Πενθεσίλεια παραγίνεται Τρωσὶ συμμαχήσουσα, Ἄρεως μὲν θυγάτηρ, Θρᾶισσα δὲ τὸ γένος.
The Amazon Penthesileia arrives on the scene, intending to act as ally to the Trojans. She is the daughter of Ares and is Thracian by birth.

> *Tabula Veronensis* II: Πενθεσίληα Ἀμαζὼν παραγίνεται.

> Apollodorus *Epitome* 5.1: ὅτι Πενθεσίλεια, Ὀτρηρῆς καὶ Ἄρεος ἀκουσίως Ἱππολύτην κτείνασα καὶ ὑπὸ Πριάμου καθαρθεῖσα... (Penthesileia, daughter of Otrera and Ares, having accidentally killed Hippolyta and been purified by Priam) ...

For Amazons in general and Penthesileia in particular, see A. Mayor, *The Amazons: Lives and Legends of Warrior Women across the Ancient World* (Princeton 2014) 287–304. Apollodorus' extra details on Penthesileia's parentage and the immediate cause of her visit to Priam are probably derived from the *Aethiopis*, as R. Wagner (*Curae Mythographicae de Apollodori fontibus* [Leipzig 1891] 207–208) surmised. We find again in Diodorus Siculus II 46.5 and Servius *ad* Vergil *Aeneid* I 491 (2.226 ed. Harv.) the picture of unintentional homicide perpetrated by Penthesileia. Furthermore, the general motif of exile caused by accidental murder is exceedingly widespread (Wagner [208n1] cites nine examples from Apollodorus alone: I 8.5, II 3.1, II 4.6.4, II 4.12, II 6.2, II 7.6.3, II 8.3.4, III 12.1–2, III 13.8.4; for other specimens of the motif in early poetry cf. *Iliad* II 661–670, XV 431–432, XVI 573–576, XXIII 87–92, XXIV 480–482; *Odyssey* xv 224; [Hesiod] *The Shield* 11–13, 80–85). The idea of purification for homicide certainly appeared at a later stage of the *Aethiopis* in connection with Achilles' killing of Thersites: see page 56 below.

A still fuller account of the circumstances of Penthesileia's arrival at Troy is to be found in Quintus Smyrnaeus I 18–32:

καὶ τότε Θερμώδοντος ἀπ' εὐρυπόροιο ῥεέθρων
ἤλυθε Πενθεσίλεια θεῶν ἐπιειμένη εἶδος,
ἄμφω καὶ στονόεντος ἐελδομένη πολέμοιο
καὶ μέγ' ἀλευομένη στυγερὴν καὶ ἀεικέα φήμην,
μή τις ἑὸν κατὰ δῆμον ἐλεγχείηισι χαλέψηι
ἀμφὶ κασιγνήτης, ἧς εἵνεκα πένθος ἄεξεν,
Ἱππολύτης· τὴν γάρ ῥα κατέκτανε δουρὶ κραταιῶι,
οὐ μὲν δή τι ἑκοῦσα, τιτυσκομένη δ' ἐλάφοιο·
τοὔνεκ' ἄρα Τροίης ἐρικυδέος ἵκετο γαῖαν.
πρὸς δ' ἔτι οἱ τόδε θυμὸς ἀρήϊος ὁρμαίνεσκεν,
ὄφρα καθηραμένη περὶ λύματα λυγρὰ φόνοιο
σμερδαλέας θυέεσσιν Ἐριννύας ἱλάσηται,
αἵ οἱ ἀδελφειῆς κεχολωμέναι αὐτίχ' ἕποντο
ἄφραστοι· κεῖναι γὰρ ἀεὶ περὶ ποσσὶν ἀλιτρῶν
στρωφῶντ', οὐδέ τιν' ἐστὶ θεᾶς ἀλιτόνθ' ὑπαλύξαι.

Here the Apollodorean details are elaborated, especially with the unique suggestion that Hippolyta was Penthesileia's sister and the consequent lurid picture of the Erinyes-tormented Amazon queen. Precisely how much ultimately derives from the *Aethiopis* one would not like to say, but the chances are high that our epic underlies these later treatments, especially Quintus' very detailed account (cf. Francis Vian, *Recherches sur les "Posthomerica" de Quintus de Smyrne* [Paris 1959] 18; Vian, Budé text i.13n2).

Priam and the Amazons are mentioned together in the *Iliad* in a context that some scholars have found incompatible with the *Aethiopis*'s presentation of Penthesileia as summarized by Proclus. At *Iliad* III 184–189 Priam is recalling an earlier encounter with the Amazons:

ἤδη καὶ Φρυγίην εἰσήλυθον ἀμπελόεσσαν
ἔνθα ἴδον πλείστους Φρύγας ἀνέρας αἰολοπώλους,
λαοὺς Ὀτρῆος καὶ Μυγδόνος ἀντιθέοιο,
οἵ ῥα τότ' ἐστρατόωντο παρ' ὄχθας Σαγγαρίοιο·
καὶ γὰρ ἐγὼν ἐπίκουρος ἐὼν μετὰ τοῖσιν ἐλέχθην
ἤματι τῶι ὅτε τ' ἦλθον Ἀμαζόνες ἀντιάνειραι.

Here, in accord with the more familiar tradition, Penthesileia (or at least her family) is located at Thermodon on the Pontus (a detail derived from our epic by

Welcker; Gruppe, *Gr. Myth.* 1.680n1, etc.). Focke (1951:336; cf. E. J. Forsdyke, *Greece before Homer: Ancient Chronology and Mythology* [London 1956] 104–105) asserts that the *Aethiopis*'s presentation of a Thracian Penthesilea[2] was inconsistent with and later than the *Iliad*'s. Kullmann's attempt (1960:46) to refute this suggestion is not very impressive.

It is more helpful to follow Wagner (*Curae Mythographicae*, 208) in recurring to the passage from Quintus of Smyrna: if the tradition of Penthesileia's exile therein contained derives from the *Aethiopis*, as he suggests, it will presumably have been intended to reconcile *Iliad* and *Aethiopis*: as a result of her exile the Amazon queen comes to help the former enemies of her family.

Severyns (1928:315) detects two further potential references by ancient critics to our poem's presentation of Penthesileia and the Amazons. The first concerns Aristarchus' contrast of Homer's ignorance of κέλητες with the knowledge displayed by οἱ νεώτεροι, which might, he thinks, presuppose that the Amazons of the *Aethiopis*, like those in sixth-century art, fought on horseback. The second relates to the Aristarchean interpretation of ἀντιάνειρα in Homer as meaning ἴσανδρος (see Apollonius the Sophist and *Etymologicum Magnum s.v.*). The great critic refused to translate the word as "opposed to men" (the meaning assigned to it by οἱ νεώτεροι) because he maintained that Homer was unaware of Amazons who opposed men in this manner. Do the νεώτεροι here included the composer of the *Aethiopis*?

καὶ κτείνει αὐτὴν ἀριστεύουσαν Ἀχιλλεύς.
Achilles kills her in the midst of her aristeia.

Tabula Veronensis II: Ἀχιλλεύς Πενθεσίλην ἀποκτείνει.

Apollodorus *Epitome* 5.1: μάχης γενομένης πολλοὺς κτείνει, ἐν οἷς καὶ Μαχάονα· εἶθ' ὕστερον θνήισκει ὑπὸ Ἀχιλλέως (A battle takes place in which she kills many adversaries, among them Machaon. Then she is killed by Achilles).

Again one is tempted (compare Wagner, *Curae Mythographicae* 207–208) to assume that the *Aethiopis* is Apollodorus' ultimate warrant for enriching Penthesileia's ἀριστεία with the death of Machaon. We should not be deterred here by the different datings of that event provided by *Ilias Parva* (see **F7**) and other sources, and still less by Proclus' failure to mention the detail. He (or his abbreviator) follows the *Ilias Parva*'s scheme of things and therefore has Machaon heal Philoctetes' wound in his synopsis of that poem's contents (ἰαθεὶς δὲ οὗτος ὑπὸ

---

[2] Robert (*Heldensage* 2.1176n1) prefers to suppose that Θρᾶισσα τὸ γένος merely refers to the homeland of Penthesileia's father, Ares.

Μαχάονος). He must consequently omit all mention of Machaon's death from his summary of the *Aethiopis* as part of the general process of eliminating such contradictions and inconsistencies. As with Memnon and Antilochus (page 61 below), the future victim of Achilles must first be elevated by a description of her own daring deeds. Quintus Smyrnaeus I 238–246 includes Podarces among the Greeks who fall before Penthesileia's onslaught.

The clash of Greeks and Amazons at Troy was a popular subject for vase painters, and Achilles and Penthesileia can often be deduced by context or firmly identified thanks to labels. The essential reference book is, of course, Deitrich von Bothmer's *Amazons in Greek Art* (Oxford 1957). See in particular pages 70–80 on Attic black-figure vases depicting the battle on foot, 80–84 for Attic black-figure representations of mounted strife, and 192–193 on early classical and classical Attic red-figure vase paintings of Achilles and Penthesileia. See too *LIMC* I.1, *s.v.* "Achilleus," no. 719. On the picture that gives the Penthesileia Painter his name see page 51 below.

Our own limited concern, of course, is to discover whether these artifacts can tell us anything new about the *Aethiopis*. On the whole, the answer must be no. It is indeed interesting and suggestive that the occasional vase painting links its Amazons with the story of Memnon. Thus on a black-figure neck-amphora in Brussels (A130: *ABV* 308.82) "the painter," to borrow von Bothmer's words (95), "has added a negro archer—an attendant of Memnon—and the Amazons become followers of Penthesileia. In the *Aethiopis* Memnon arrived *after* the death of Penthesileia, and one would not expect to find the Ethiopian contingents mixing with the Amazonian, but the point need not be pressed." On an alabastron in Berlin (inv. 3382: *ARV²* 269) the scene is divided between a black individual and an Amazon so that the former helps identify the latter as a companion of Penthesileia. But whether this type of connection was meant to do anything more than facilitate just such an identification one may very much doubt.

A fine example of what sort of illumination *not* to expect from these vases is provided by the efforts of earlier scholars (bibliography in Rzach 1922: 2397.59–2398.18)[3] to segregate as representative of the *Aethiopis*'s version those specimens that portray the Amazons fighting on horseback. As Rzach himself clearly saw (1922:2398.10–18), the factors that determine whether a given vase's Amazonomachy takes place on foot, on horseback, in chariots, or in varying combinations of the aforementioned modes of war are largely artistic, matters of "das freie Walten einer künstlerischer Phantasie," and the painter's concern

---

[3] Add e.g. Robert, *Heldensage* 2.1177n3; cf. R. Heinze, *Virgils epische Technik* (Leipzig 1908) 198 = *Vergil's Epic Technique* (Berkeley 1993) 159.

for balance and symmetry in his composition. More recently A. Kossatz-Deissmann has reminded us, in connection with depictions of Antilochus in the act of hepatoscopy ("Nestor und Antilochus: Zu den spätarchaischen Bildern mit Leberschau," *Archäologischer Anzeiger* 96 [1981]: 570–571: see page 63 below), that vase painters often conceive their mythical subject matter in contemporary terms: "The Greek habit was to present myth history in modern dress" (Boardman, *Classical Quarterly* 23 [1973]: 197).

Thersites

καὶ κτείνει αὐτήν ἀριστεύουσαν Ἀχιλλεύς, οἱ δέ Τρῶες αὐτὴν θάπτουσι. καὶ Ἀχιλλεὺς Θερσίτην ἀναιρεῖ, λοιδορηθεὶς πρὸς αὐτοῦ καὶ ὀνειδισθεὶς τὸν ἐπὶ τῆι Πενθεσιλείαι λεγόμενον ἔρωτα ...

(Achilles kills Penthesileia...) and the Trojans bury her. And Achilles slays Thersites because he had been insulted by that individual and reviled by him for his alleged love for Penthesileia.

> Apollodorus *Epitome* 5.1: εἴθ' ὕστερον θνήισκει ὑπὸ Ἀχιλλέως, ὅστις μετὰ θάνατον ἐρασθεὶς τῆς Ἀμαζόνος κτείνει Θερσίτην λοιδοροῦντα αὐτόν (Then afterwards Penthesileia is killed by Achilles, and he, after her death, falls in love with the Amazon, and kills Thersites for insulting him).

E. Howald (*Der Dichter der Ilias* [Zurich 1946] 127) thinks that the tradition of Achilles' combat with Penthesileia is (in contrast to that of his combat with Memnon) old and early: he compares the exploits of Heracles and Theseus against Amazons. But what of the sequel? In later accounts (most explicitly Quintus Smyrnaeus I 643–674) Achilles kills Penthesileia and then falls in love with her.[4]

> μέγα δ' ἄχνυτο Πηλέος υἱὸς
> κούρης εἰσορόων ἐρατὸν σθένος ἐν κονίηισι·
> τοὔνεκά οἱ κραδίην ὀλοαὶ κατέδαπτον ἀνῖαι,
> ὁππόσον ἀμφ' ἑτάροιο πάρος Πατρόκλοιο δαμέντος.
>
> Quintus Smyrnaeus I 718–721

In other words, Achilles' feelings of pity and love and his killing of Thersites all occur over Penthesileia's corpse.[5]

---

[4] Late authors import an element of necrophily: see Vian on Quintus Smyrnaeus I 644–670 (Budé i.40n2).

[5] For other late authors who reproduce this scheme see Vian's Budé text of Quintus Smyrnaeus i.1n3.

Figure 6. Red-figure cup, interior: Achilles kills the Amazon Penthesileia.
Attributed to the Penthesileia Painter, ca. 500–450 BCE.
Munich, Antikensammlungen 2688. Drawing after A. Fürtwangler and
K. Reichhold, *Griechische Vasenmalerei: Auswahl hervorragender Vasenbilder*
(Munich 1904), Tafel 6.

The feelings of pity and love may perhaps be implied in the famous vase painting whose artist takes his modern title from the Amazon queen (Munich 2688: *ARV*^{2} 879.1 = *LIMC* I.1, *s.v.* "Achilleus," no. 733 = VII.1, *s.v.* "Penthesileia," no. 34: see Figure 6). Here the glances exchanged by the Greek warrior and the dying Amazon have been interpreted as indicative of nascent love between Achilles and Penthesileia (so e.g. Rzach 1922:2397.42–58; Ed. Fraenkel, *Due seminari romani* [*Sussidi Eruditi* 28 (1977)] 68). Against this we must set the skepticism of Bothmer (*Amazons in Greek Art*, 148: "he has put much intensity into the faces, but who is to say whether the expressions reflect love or hate, remorse or reproach, or other emotions?") and his even more stern reminder (147) that the specifying of the Amazon as Penthesileia and the Greek as Achilles lacks any actual evidence. But the analogous instances of "intensive Blickbeziehung" which U. Hausmann cites ("Antikentausch Louvre-Tübingen," *Archäologischer Anzeiger* 80 [1965]: 162) from probable depictions of the same scene favor the traditional view.

Now if we believe Proclus (and there seems no reason to distrust him),[6] things were presented differently in the *Aethiopis*: Penthesileia's body had been consigned to the earth by the Trojans[7] before Thersites ever taunted Achilles. The incident as thus portrayed would seem to have been more illuminating for the mentality of Thersites than for Achilles, and we need take the contents of the former's railery no more seriously than we do the equivalent attack upon the character of Agamemnon in *Iliad* II 225–244. Cf. E. Rohde, *Der griechische Roman und seine Vorläufer*[3] (Leipzig 1914) 110n2: "Wer sagt denn, ob das 'Gerede' wahr gewesen" (with Proclus' τὸν ... λεγόμενον ἔρωτα contrast Apollodorus' phrasing with its implication that Achilles *was* in love). We need not, then, follow the extreme reactions of such earlier scholars as Bethe (1922:146: "Diese raffinirte, ja perverse Verwendung, für das heroische Epos unmöglich"),[8] in denying the incident to our epic.

Severyns (1925:159) makes the ingenious suggestion that the apparently humane and chivalrous attitude which the *Aethiopis*'s Achilles displayed towards

---

[6]   Vian (Budé text of Quintus Smyrnaeus i.7), however, alleges that the sequence here remarked upon was forced on Proclus by "la commodité de l'exposition" (i.e. Penthesileia's burial, if mentioned at any other stage, would interrupt the sequence "abuse–murder–purification"). Similarly West 2013:141: "narrative convenience."

[7]   *Achilles* buried Penthesileia, according to later authors (see Vian's Budé text of Quintus Smyrnaeus i.164). The version followed by the *Aethiopis* is perhaps preserved by Quintus of Smyrna I 782–810, when he says Priam persuaded the Atreidae to allow the Trojans to recover and bury Penthesileia.

[8]   It is most inconsistent of Bethe to adopt this attitude, and yet also to argue that the original epic version may be recovered from Σ Sophocles *Philoctetes* 445: φονευθεύσης τῆς Πενθεσιλείας ὑπὸ Ἀχιλλέως ὁ Θερσίτης δόρατι, ἔπληξε τὸν ὀφθαλμὸν αὐτῆς· διὸ ὀργισθεὶς ὁ Ἀχιλλεὺς κονδύλωι [Brunck; -οις codd.] αὐτὸν ἀνεῖλεν· ἐλέγετο γὰρ [ὅτι del. Lloyd-Jones] καὶ μετὰ θάνατον ἐρασθεὶς αὐτῆς συνεληλύθεναι [-ἐλήλυθεν Papageorgiou]; cf. Tzetzes *ad* Lycophron 999 (2.312 Scheer). If we follow the implications of Bethe's own approach, we must surely conclude that this version's combination of sadism and the erotic takes us a further step from archaic epic. This approach may, indeed, be wrong and the scholion's details may derive from a genuinely early tradition (so e.g. Fraenkel, *Due seminari romani*, 57: "la scena di crudeltà è la piu antica, l'altra [in Proclus' summary] è una volgarizzazione posteriore": contra Robert, *Heldensage* 2.1179: "später hat man die Geschichte immer krasser ausgemalt"). But this does not entail that the *Aethiopis* employed the more ancient version of events, and Proclus' phrasing certainly seems to exclude any such connection with the version just outlined. The refinement that Penthesileia's beauty was only revealed when her helmet was removed (Propertius III.11.15–16, Quintus I 630 and 657), derived from the *Aethiopis* by West (2013:141), seems to me to belong to later combinations of sadism and the erotic.

his fallen enemy represents a development of the more courteous and sympathetic facets of the hero's character as brought out in his encounter with Priam in the last book of the *Iliad*. Cf. E. Christian Kopff's comparable hypothesis in *ANRW* II.31.2:93 and then in *The Greek Renaissance of the Eighth Century B.C.: Tradition and Innovation* (Stockholm 1983) 60–61.

καὶ Ἀχιλλεὺς Θερσίτην ἀναιρεῖ ... καὶ ἐκ τούτου στάσις γίνεται τοῖς Ἀχαιοῖς περὶ τοῦ Θερσίτου φόνου.

(Achilles slays Thersites...) and after this act, a dispute arises among the Greeks, concerning the killing of Thersites.

On the general phenomenon of Thersites see H. Usener, "Der Stoff des griechischen Epos," *Sitzungsberichte der Kaiserlichen Akademie der Wissenschaften in Wien, Philosophisch-Historische Classe* 137 (1897): 42–63 = *Kleine Schriften* (Leipzig 1912–1913) 4.239–259; H. D. Rankin, "Thersites the Malcontent: A Discussion," *Symbolae Osloenses* 47 (1972): 36–70. On the specific question of the relationship between the scenes in the *Iliad* and the *Aethiopis* in which Thersites featured see W. Kullmann, "Die Probe des Achaierheeres in der *Ilias*," *Museum Helveticum* 12 (1955): 253–273 = *Homerische Motive*, 38–63; Ø. Andersen, "Thersites und Thoas vor Troia," *Symbolae Osloenses* 57 (1982): 19–34.

It has long been recognized that the events described in *Iliad* II 212–277 bear a close resemblance to what may be inferred from the present part of Proclus' summary. In both, Thersites rails against a Greek leader and is punished by a blow. This blow, of course, is fatal only in the case of the *Aethiopis* episode: does this entail that the motifs are "primary" in that epic? Several scholars have assumed so, Kullmann in particular. His argument is more specific than most, since he believes that Thersites' speech at 225–242 derives closely from the parallel scene in the *Aethiopis*, where the charge πλεῖαί τοι χαλκοῦ κλισίαι, πολλαὶ δὲ γυναῖκες | εἰσὶν ἐνὶ κλισίηις ἐξαίρετοι κτλ. will have been leveled by the malcontent against Achilles. This last supposition is most unlikely, since for many years it has been clear that the immediate inspiration for this particular speech lies much closer to hand, in book I of the *Iliad* itself. Thersites' harangue "apes," as it were, Achilles' complaints against Agamemnon in *Iliad* I 149–171 (see especially D. Lohmann, *Die Komposition der Reden in der* Ilias [Berlin 1970] 175–178: cf. Andersen 1978:25–26).

May the more general hypothesis of Iliadic dependence upon the *Aethiopis* still stand? It is true that the latter poem employs the motifs in a more "tragic" manner (at least as far as Thersites is concerned) and in a simpler fashion (Thersites is punished by the hero against whom he rails: in the *Iliad* Odysseus beats him for blackguarding Agamemnon). But as we saw above in the context of a more general discussion (page 10), and as Andersen shows here in great detail (1978:23–24), the presence of elaboration and the absence of "tragic" consequences are no infallible indexes of derivative status. Even the reference to Achilles in *Iliad* II 220 (ἔχθιστος δ' Ἀχιλῆϊ μάλιστ' ἦν [scil. Θερσίτης] ἠδ' Ὀδυσῆϊ) need not be the telltale vestige of the story's original form it is so often assumed to be: ὁ γὰρ τοῖς ἀρίστοις ἔχθιστος χείριστος, as Eustathius 204.38 (1.312 Van der Valk) saw:[9] this obvious antithesis tells us nothing. If Thersites were "ein sprechender Name" ("the valiant one") interpreted κατ' ἀντίφρασιν (see Andersen 1978:25 and 33n48), his presence at Troy might perhaps be an Homeric invention. But there is no need for such an interpretation of κατ' ἀντίφρασιν: see H. von Kamptz, *Homerische Personennamen: Sprachwissenschaftliche und historische Klassifikation* (Göttingen 1982) 236 for the name as probably deriving from θράσος (pejoratively meant).

There are indeed differences between the Iliadic and the *Aethiopis*'s scenes which cannot be explained in terms of their interdependence. Thersites is introduced at *Iliad* II 212–221 without mention of father or birthplace—a sure sign of his low origin (cf. Σ bT *ad loc.* [1.228 Erbse]: εὖ δὲ καὶ οὐκ ἀπὸ πατρὸς αὐτὸν συνέστησεν, οὐδ' ἀπὸ πατρίδος, ἀλλ' ἀπὸ τοῦ τρόπου μόνου καὶ τῆς μορφῆς). His unpopularity with the Greek army is indicated by the general contentment induced by the drubbing Odysseus administers (274–275: νῦν δὲ τόδε μέγ' ἄριστον ἐν Ἀργείοισιν ἔρεξεν, | ὅς τὸν λωβητῆρα ἐπεσβόλον ἔσχ' ἀγοράων). Yet in the *Aethiopis*, we are assured, his death caused an uproar. It is hard not to associate this otherwise inexplicable fact with the un-Homeric tradition of an Aetolian Thersites of noble birth, son of Oineus' brother Agrius and kinsman of Diomedes: cf. Σ A *Iliad* II 212: Οἰνεὺς καὶ Ἄγριος ἀδελφοί ὡς λέγει ὁ ποιητὴς ἐν τῆι Θ. ἀλλ' ὁ μὲν Οἰνεὺς ἦν πατὴρ Μελεάγρου, ὁ δὲ Ἄγριος Θερσίτου, μήτηρ δὲ Θερσίτου Δῖα; Σ bT: Ἀγρίου δὲ καὶ Δίας τῆς Πορθάονος αὐτὸν φασιν. εἰ δὲ συγγενὴς ἦν Διομήδους, οὐκ ἂν αὐτὸν ἔπληξεν Ὀδυσσεύς· τοὺς γὰρ ἰδιώτας μόνον ἔτυπτεν; Eustathius 204.6–8 (1.311 Van der Valk), etc.

A more specific account of what Proclus calls a στάσις is given by Quintus Smyrnaeus I 767–771, where Diomedes, alone of the Greeks, is incensed at the killing of his kinsman. This has been taken to derive from the *Aethiopis* by, for instance, Kullmann (1960:86) and Vian *ad loc.* (i.42n1), but the difficulties of reconciling this picture with the wider implications of an Aetolian Thersites

---

[9]   Cf. Σ b *Iliad* II 220 (1.231 Erbse): τοῖς οὖν καλλίστος ἐναντίος ὁ ἔχθιστος, "die giftige krote ihren Geifer gegen die Besten spuckt" (Wilamowitz, *Ilias und Homer*, 271n2), etc. Severyns (1928:316) postulates a now-lost note by Aristarchus which took the *Iliad*'s ἔχθιστος δ' Ἀχιλῆϊ to be the starting point for the *Aethiopis*'s fatal development of the pair's antagonism. Cf. van Thiel 2014:2.196.

(as one of the sons of Agrius who first imprison and then kill Diomedes' father Oeneus: cf. Apollodorus *Epitome* 1.8.6) are well conveyed by Andersen (1982:19–20; cf. 1978:20).[10] The notion that the *Aethiopis* involved Diomedes in this way or that it indulged in any great detail over the Aetolian background is very uncertain. There are, indeed, other details within the outline provided by Proclus' summary which we are quite unable to fill in from later accounts in literature or art (on the latter see *LIMC* I.1, *s.v.* "Achilleus," 171–172). Was Thersites, if not the unpopular misfit of Homeric fame, at least as misshapen?[11] How exactly was he killed by Achilles? Quintus of Smyrna has him dispatched by an exceptionally severe boxing of the ear (I 742–747).[12] The Capitoline Tabula (see page 98 below) seems to show Achilles brandishing a weapon against Thersites. A normal weapon finishes him off in other authors (cf. Vian's Budé text of Quintus Smyrnaeus i.164), and the famous red-figure Apulian vase now in Boston (03.804: *Red-Figured Vases of Apulia* II.113 [no. 17/75] = *LIMC* I.1, *s.v.* "Achilleus," no. 794) depicts the beheaded corpse of Thersites. Attempts to decide priority between these versions are inconclusive (the former derivative and presupposing the Iliadic drubbing: J. Ebert, "Die Gestalt des Thersites in der Ilias," *Philologus* 113 (1969): 169n6; the weapon a "secondary normalisation": Andersen 1982:33n45). That the Capitoline Tabula Iliaca perhaps shows Thersites killed at the tomb of Penthesileia is doubtless artist's shorthand; the building in front of which Thersites lies on the Boston vase mentioned above is merely one of a number of problems posed by that artifact.[13]

---

[10] Kullmann's thesis (1960:305–306) that the *Iliad* depicts an "Animosität" harbored by Diomedes against Achilles, and that this "Animosität" is to be explained in terms of the former's anger against the latter as depicted in the *Aethiopis*'s treatment of Thersites' death, is exploded by Andersen (1982:19–21).

[11] Cf. Pherecydes *FGrHist* 3 F123: Φ. δὲ καὶ τοῦτον ἕνα τῶν ἐπὶ τὸν Καλυδώνιον κάπρον στρατευ-σάντων φησίν. ἐκκλίνοντα δὲ τὴν τοῦ συὸς μάχην ὑπὸ Μελεάγρου κατακρημνισθῆναι· διὸ καὶ λελωβῆσθαι τὸ σῶμα. This seems to maintain the Aetolian tradition (see page 54). But, as Andersen says (32n32), it may merely represent an attempt to account for the Homeric deformity.

[12] Vian *ad loc.* (1.164) assumes that this reflects the *Aethiopis*'s version.

[13] For a full description of which see Cambidoglou and Trendall *ad loc.* (*Red-Figured Vases of Apulia* II.172). Achilles reposes on an elaborate couch and Phoenix seems to display grief, while to the right Diomedes with an Aetolian soldier is restrained by Menelaus and to the left Agamemnon and Phorbas hurry to calm the situation. As the two scholars cited above conclude, "the scene depicted is unique in vase-painting and is based upon some legend of the Trojan War, perhaps recorded in one of the lost Cyclic poems or related to the *Achilles Thersitoctonus* of Chaeremon" (*TrGF* I.17–218 [Sn.]). Even more mysterious is another Apulian vase (Taranto 52265: *Red-Figured Vases of Apulia* I.[2]25) showing Thersites in the company of, for instance, Helen (who holds an egg), Odysseus. and one of the Dioscuri. The labeled Thersites is not at all deformed, indeed (to quote Cambidoglou and Trendall I.40–41), "his pose has a very statuesque look." But it would be rash to follow Kullmann (1960:147n2) in associating the scene with an unattested tradition of Thersites as a suitor of Helen (for all that Aphrodite and Eros survey the scene).

μετὰ δὲ ταῦτα Ἀχιλλεὺς εἰς Λέσβον πλεῖ, καὶ θύσας Ἀπόλλωνι, καὶ Ἀρτέμιδι, καὶ Λητοῖ καθαίρεται τοῦ φόνου ὑπ' Ὀδυσσέως.
And after this, Achilles sails to Lesbos, and, after sacrificing to Apollo and Artemis and Leto, is purified by Odysseus from his act of murder.

This scene has long been regarded as an important stage in the development of Greek ideas concerning pollution and purification, concepts which are so conspicuous by their near absence from Homer's poems,[14] and so predominant in other early epics (see the list of relevant passages in Lloyd-Jones, *The Justice of Zeus* [Berkeley 1971] 73) and later literature. Since Rohde (1886.1:272 = 180 [Engl. transl.]), we have come to see that the issue is far more complex than was once supposed, and that such crucial notions as καθάρσις or μίασμα are unlikely to have sprung up overnight in an interval between Homer and the *Aethiopis*. Indeed, passages like *Iliad* I 314 (the Greeks after the plague ἀπελυμαίνοντο καὶ εἰς ἅλα λύματα βάλλον) and *Odyssey* xxii 480–484 (the use of brimstone to purify the hall after the slaying of the suitors) provide *prima facie* evidence that Homer was acquainted with purifications that "are thought of as cathartic in the magical sense" (to quote E. R. Dodds, *The Greeks and the Irrational* [Berkeley 1951] 54n39). So instead of treating literature as a direct and simple reflection of contemporary beliefs and attitudes, we should learn to appreciate that poems are works of art with their own sophisticated inhibitions and rules as to which portions of reality to include and omit. This has nowhere been perceived more clearly than in the book of Lloyd-Jones cited above, which contains an excellent discussion of the significance of pollution and purification in archaic Greek literature (together with a full evaluation of previous scholars' treatments). Note in particular its insistence that

> we should surely expect the belief in pollution to be something ancient, something far older than any extant literature, older perhaps than any literature whatever. ... Can it be that the notions of pollution and purification play a minor part in Homer not because they were unimportant in the early period, but because the epic poets did not choose to allow them any prominent place in the world depicted in their poems? ... The *Iliad* and *Odyssey* are not literal reproductions of life but works of poetic fiction, whose authors were at liberty to give or refuse prominence to any belief or practice according to their pleasure. The dark,

---

[14] As observed by Aristarchus (cf. Severyns 1928:139–140). Note especially the tone of Σ T *Iliad* XI 690 (3.261 Erbse): καὶ παρ' Ὁμήρωι οὐκ οἴδαμεν φονέα καθαιρόμενον, ἀλλ' ἀντιτίνοντα ἢ φυγαδευόμενον.

the daemonic, the numinous side of religion is on any view surprisingly absent from the Homeric poems.

(70–76)

See further R. Parker, *Miasma: Pollution and Purification in Early Greece* (Oxford 1983) 138 and 131n102 on our passage's importance as a document for these ideas.

For Apollo, Artemis, and Leto as a common trinity in cult see Nisbet-Hubbard on Horace *Odes* 1.21.1. Why does this particular trio of deities feature here? Apollo's appropriateness seems obvious, but it is important to stress that this is the only passage in ancient literature where he is specifically *a recipient of offerings* in the context of purification for murder. See W. H. Roscher in Roscher *s.v.* "Apollon," 1.441–442; Farnell, *Cults of the Greek States* (Oxford 1907) 4:293, and especially R. R. Dyer, "The Evidence for Apolline Purification Rituals at Delphi and Athens," *Journal of Hellenic Studies* 89 (1969): 40 on the god's various connections with purification. His role in Aeschylus' *Eumenides* is clearly relevant but not strictly comparable since in the case of Orestes he assumes the position of the human purifier.[15]

"It was probably as the sister of Apollo that Artemis became a goddess of purification," as Farnell (2:467) observes, citing the very passage under discussion. She often heals victims of madness: see J. Mannes, *Der Wahnsinn im griechischen Mythos und in der Dichtung bis zum Drama des fünften Jahrhunderts* (Heidelberg 1970) 42–43; H. Lloyd-Jones, "Artemis and Iphigeneia," *Journal of Hellenic Studies* 103 (1983): 96–97 = *Academic Papers* [II], 321–322. For further light on her appearance here we may note the stress upon the purity of Artemis in such contexts as Euripides *Hippolytus* 73–81 and 1437–1439 or in *Iphigenia in Tauris* 380–384. But as with her brother, there is no other direct evidence for her connection with purification from murder. Analogies with this connection may perhaps reside in her curing of the Proetids in Bacchylides 11.85–103 (a deed that is certainly presented as an act of purification on the Canicattini crater [Syracuse 47038: *LIMC* VII.1, B5 (p. 524): cf. G. Schneider-Herrmann, "Das Geheimnis der Artemis in Etrurien," *Antike Kunst* 13 (1970): 59–60 and plate 30.2]). One should also remember that Pherecydes *FGrHist* 3 F135[a] locates Orestes' return to sanity in a temple of Artemis (ὁ δὲ καταφεύγει εἰς τὸ ἱερὸν τῆς Ἀρτέμιδος καὶ ἵζει ἱκέτης πρὸς τῶι βωμῶι. αἱ δὲ Ἐρινύες ἔρχονται ἐπ' αὐτὸν θέλουσαι ἀποκτεῖναι, καὶ ἐρύκει αὐτὰς ἡ Ἄρτεμις).

Much of what appears above as puzzling would be far less so if there were an important cult of Apollo, Artemis, and Leto on Lesbos at the time of the *Aethiopis*'s composition. On Apollo's importance on Lesbos see Farnell, *Cults of*

---

[15]   The difference is emphasized by, for instance, Nilsson *GGR*[2] 1.146–147 and Dyer.

the Greek States 4:162–163. On Alcaeus' hymns to Apollo and Artemis see Page, *Sappho and Alcaeus: An Introduction to the Study of Ancient Lesbian Poetry* (Oxford 1955) 244–252 and 261–265. For Achilles and Lesbos see West 2013:143.

Odysseus' task as purifier is interesting: his position within the *Aethiopis*'s voyage to Lesbos has reminded some scholars of his function in the visit to Chryse in *Iliad* I 308–311 and 430–445, and Kullmann (1960:101) characteristically sees the latter epic as specifically copying the former. It is perhaps more to the point to speak in terms of Odysseus' tendency in epic to occupy the important role of resolver of threatening strife.

Memnon

Μέμνων δὲ ὁ Ἠοῦς υἱὸς ἔχων ἡφαιστότευκτον πανοπλίαν παραγίνεται τοῖς Τρωσὶ βοηθήσων.

And Memnon, the son of the Dawn goddess, arrives on the scene with armor fashioned by Hephaestus, intent on helping the Trojans.

> Apollodorus *Epitome* 5.3: Μέμνων δὲ ὁ Τιθωνοῦ καὶ Ἠοῦς πολλὴν Αἰθιό-πων δύναμιν ἀθροίσας παραγίνεται[16] (And Memnon, the son of Tithonus and the Dawn goddess, after assembling a large force of Ethiopians, arrives on the scene).

The marriage of Eos and Tithonus is implied by the Homeric formula Ἠὼς δ' ἐκ λεχέων παρ' ἀγαυοῦ Τιθωνοῖο | ὄρνυθ' ἵν' ἀθανάτοισι φόως φέροι ἠδὲ βροτοῖσι (*Iliad* XI 1–2 = *Odyssey* v 1–2). But the notion of immortality freely (if disastrously) bestowable upon humans which the story as a whole entails is so alien to Homer's outlook (see Griffin 1977:42 = *Oxford Readings in Homer's* Iliad [Oxford 2001] 372) that no more is said of Memnon's father in *Iliad* or *Odyssey* (except for the appearance of his name in the list of Priam's brothers at *Iliad* XX 237), and the earliest attested mention of Tithonus' unfortunate form of immortality is at *Homeric Hymn to Aphrodite* 218 (on which see Faulkener *ad loc.* and index *s.v.*; J. Th. Kakridis, "Die Pelopssage bei Pindar," *Philologus* 85 [1930]: 463–477 = Μελέτες καὶ Ἄρθρα, ed. Polites [Athens 1971] 55–68 = *Pindaros und Bakchylides* (*Wege der Forschung* 134 [1970]) 175; and F. Preisshofen, *Untersuchungen zur Darstellung des Greisenalters in der frühgriechischen Dichtung* [*Hermes Einzelschriften* 34 (1977)] 13–20). On Tithonus in general see J. Kakridis, "Tithonus," *Wiener Studien* 48 (1930): 25–38; Cook, *Zeus: A Study in Ancient Religion* (Cambridge 1940) 3.24; R. G. M. Nisbet and M. Hubbard, *A Commentary on Horace Odes Book 1* (Oxford 1969) 326–327; and D. D. Boedeker, *Aphrodite's Entry into Greek Epic* (*Mnemosyne* Suppl. 32 [1974]) 95.

---

[16] On the constitution of the text here see Wagner's Teubner edition[2] (*Addenda*) p. 270 on 203.3–9.

Apart from the reference to Antilochus' death at *Odyssey* iv 186–189 (see page 61 below), Memnon himself is mentioned in *Odyssey* xi 522, where Odysseus reassures the spirit of Achilles that his son Neoptolemus was a great warrior in all respects: κεῖνον δὴ κάλλιστον ἴδον μετὰ Μέμνονα δῖον (Memnon's beauty[17] was inherited from both father [cf. *Homeric Hymn to Aphrodite* 225; Tyrtaeus fr. 12.5W; etc.] and mother [who is καλή in *Iliad* IX 707 and art generally (page 35n11 above)]). An unreliable source appears to imply that Memnon's tomb was referred to by "Hesiod" (fr. dub. 353 MW). The single line δουρῖ δὲ ξυστῶι μέμανεν Αἴας αἱμαῆι τε Μέμνων is attributed to Alcman (fr. 68 *PMGF*), and Simonides is credited with a dithyramb entitled "Μέμνων" (539 P). Pindar mentions him several times (*Pythian* VI 32; *Nemean* III 63, 6.50; *Isthmian* V 41, 8.54). The school of Neonalysis naturally presumes that the poet of the *Iliad* knew about Memnon. This may be right, but Kullmann (*Göttingische Gelehrte Anzeiger* 217 [1965]: 26 = *Homerische Motive*, 187) clearly goes too far when he argues that the figure of Phaenops (*Iliad* V 152–158), a father beset by old age who is not able to welcome his sons back from the war because they are slain at Troy, is modeled on the relationship of Tithonus to Memnon. The motif of "the bereaved father is a dominant figure in the Iliadic plot from Chryses to Priam," as Griffin ("Homeric Pathos and Objectivity," *Classical Quarterly* 26 [1976]: 174 = 1980:123) observed.

The title of our epic confirms that there, as in [Hesiod] *Theogony* 984–985: Τιθωνῶι δ' Ἠὼς τέκε Μέμνονα χαλκοκορυστήν, Ἀιθιόπων βασιλῆα. As West observes *ad loc.*, their king will have led the Aethiopians to Troy from the east,[18] appropriately enough for a son of the Dawn. On the Aethiopians in early literature and art see (apart from West as cited), Lesky, "Aithiopika," *Hermes* 87 (1959): 27–38 = *Gesammelte Schriften: Aufsätze und Reden zu antiker und deutscher Dichtung und Kultur* (Bern 1966) 411; A. Dilhe, *Umstrittene Daten: Untersuchungen zum Auftreten der Griechen am Roten Meer* (Cologne 1965) 65 (cf. his article "Der fruchtbare Osten," *Rheinisches Museum* 105 [1962]: 100n6); Snowden, *Blacks in Antiquity* and *Before Colour Prejudice: The Ancient View of Blacks* (Cambridge, MA 1983) index *s.v.* "Ethiopians"; R. Engels, "Bemerkungen zum Aithiopenbild der vorhellenistischen Literatur," in *Straub Festschrift* (*Beihefte der Bonner Jahrbücher* 39 [1977]) 7.

On the origins of the story of Memnon see E. Howald, *Der Dichter der Ilias* (Zurich 1946) 127, 140–141; M. Janda, *Elysion: Entstehung und Entwicklung der*

---

[17] Sadly ignorant of the dictum "black is beautiful," the earliest authors and artists (naturally enough, in view of his parentage) represent the Aethiopian Memnon as white-skinned. See Vian, Budé text of Quintus Smyrnaeus i.165, who presumes the same was true of the *Aethiopis*, and Frank M. Snowden Jr., *Blacks in Antiquity* (Cambridge, MA 1970) 152–160 and Burgess 2001: 159–160.

[18] The size of Memnon's army is stressed by Apollodorus *Epitome* 5.3, which Vian (Budé text of Quintus Smyrnaeus i.165) derives from our epic.

griechischen Religion (Innsbruck 2005) 128–142. In the present context he was clearly intended as Achilles' foil: both heroes have a goddess as mother, and both wear armor forged by Hephaestus;[19] the death of each is closely linked with that of the other; and both are granted immortality.[20] See further Boedeker, *Aphrodite's Entry into Greek Epic*, 82, where she stresses that "the *Iliad* passage is not necessarily the most archaic context" (84) of the motif whereby solicitous mother procures divine armor for heroic son. For other objects belonging or bequeathed to heroes and fabricated by Hephaestus see *Cypria* F3 and my note *ad loc.* For the mother fetching armor for a heroic son as a folk-tale motif, see my article, "The Hero and His Arms," *Greece and Rome* 54 (2007): 145–150. Proclus' mention of Memnon's ἡφαιστότευκτος πανοπλία convinced Welcker (2:173) that this hero's divine armor had been accorded the same full description as Achilles' in *Iliad* XVIII 478–608. Welcker's guess has been accepted by numerous other scholars,[21] most notably Ed. Fraenkel (in his important article "Vergil und die Aethiopis," *Philologus* 87 [1932]: 242 = *Kleine Beiträge* 2.173), who supported it by adducing the evidence of *Aeneid* VIII 383–384 (Venus' words to Vulcan): *te filia Nerei | te potuit lacrimis Tithonia flectere coniunx*, a passage which may imply for the *Aethiopis* a scene similar to *Iliad* XVIII 457–461. The *Aeneid* suggests considerable interest in Memnon's armor; the frieze in the temple of Juno displays *Eoasque acies et nigri Memnonis arma* (I 489), while Dido questions Aeneas at I 751 as to *quibus Aurorae venisset filius armis.* Visual art did not fail to rise to the challenge: thus an elaborately armored Memnon occurs on a neck-amphora by Exekias (London B209: *ABV* 144.8 = *LIMC* VI.1, *s.v.* "Memnon," 5) with an Ethiopian attendant on either side, one holding a club and the other a shield.

καὶ Θέτις τῶι παιδὶ τὰ κατά τὸν Μέμνονα προλέγει.
Thetis tells her son [Achilles] the future as regards events relating to Memnon.

In the *Iliad*, Thetis is frequently conceived as warning her son of his future fate: most clearly in *Iliad* XVIII 94–96: τὸν δ᾽ αὖτε προσέειπε Θέτις κατὰ δάκρυ χέουσα·| "ὠκύμορος δή μοι, τέκος, ἔσσεαι, οἷ᾽ ἀγορεύεις·| αὐτίκα γάρ τοι ἔπειτα μεθ᾽ Ἕκτορα πότμος ἑτοῖμος." Achilles himself gives a slightly differing account of his mother's prophecy in IX 410–416:

μήτηρ γάρ τέ μέ φησι θεὰ Θέτις ἀργυρόπεζα
διχθαδίας κῆρας φερέμεν θανάτοιο τέλοσδε.
εἰ μέν κ᾽ αὖθι μένων Τρώων πόλιν ἀμφιμάχωμαι

---

[19] For analogies between both heroes and the figure of Rhesus see B. Fenik, *Iliad X and the Rhesus: The Myth* (Collection Latomus 73 [1964]) 34–35. As Hector's successor in the rôle of Achilles' victim he could also be said to be Hector's foil.

[20] With Proclus on Memnon's armor cf. Apollodorus *Epitome* 3.7.5.7 on Achilles' πανοπλία.

[21] E.g. Rzach 1922:2399.43–44 and 2405.8–11, Kopff, *ANRW* II.31.2:935.

ὤλετο μέν μοι νόστος, ἀτὰρ κλέος ἄφθιτον ἔσται·
εἰ δέ κεν οἴκαδ' ἵκωμι φίλην ἐς πατρίδα γαῖαν,
ὤλετο μοι κλέος ἐσθλὸν ἐπὶ δηρὸν δέ μοι αἰὼν
ἔσσεται, οὐδέ κέ μ' ὦκα τέλος θανάτοιο κιχείη.

The other Greeks are aware of Thetis' role: Nestor in XI 794–795 raises the possibility that Achilles' refusal to fight is based on some such admonition from his mother (εἴ δέ τινα φρεσὶν ᾗσι θεοπροπίην ἀλεείνει | καί τινά οἱ πὰρ Ζηνὸς ἐπέφραδε πότνια μήτηρ ...), and Patroclus (to whom Nestor addresses these words) repeats them almost verbatim to Achilles at XVI 36–37.

It is presumably some similar revelation of the future regarding Achilles' death (and consequent immortality?) that Proclus alludes to here (so Welcker 2:173;[22] cf. Kullmann 1960:37). Achilles' killing of Memnon is followed so closely by his own decease that τὰ κατὰ τὸν Μέμνονα ("the events concerning Memnon": cf. LSJ *s.v.* κατά BIV2) would be an acceptable way of referring to the latter incident as well as to the preliminary victory over Memnon.

καὶ συμβολῆς γενομένης Ἀντίλοχος ὑπὸ Μέμνονος ἀναιρεῖται.
A battle takes place and Antilochus is slain by Memnon.

Cf. Apollodorus *Epitome* 5.3: Μέμνων ... τῶν Ἑλλήνων οὐκ ὀλίγους ἀναιρεῖ, κτείνει καὶ Ἀντίλοχον (Memnon slays no small a quantity of Greeks, and then kills Antilochus).

This famous event is presupposed by *Odyssey* iv 186–188:

οὐδ' ἄρα Νέστορος υἱὸς ἀδακρύτω ἔχεν ὄσσε·
μνήσατο γὰρ κατὰ θυμὸν ἀμύμονος Ἀντιλόχοιο,
τόν ῥ' Ἠοῦς ἔκτεινε φαεινῆς ἀγλαὸς υἱός.

"Um seins Gegners Achilleus auch als Kampfer nicht unwert zu sein, musste Memnon auch seine Aristie haben" as Rzach (1922:2399.59–60) observes.

Fraenkel observed that the character of Camilla—long recognized (see "Vergil und die Aethiopis," 243 = *Kleine Beiträge* 2.174n2) and once directly identified (*Aeneid* XI 662) as analogous to that of Penthesileia—may not be the only detail in which Vergil's epic is indebted to the *Aethiopis*. In *Aeneid* X 769–793 Mezentius is retreating before Aeneas' attack, hampered by the missile trailing from his shield. Lausus, the son of Mezentius, sacrifices his own life in a futile attempt to rescue his father from the Trojan leader. The minor differences from the prototype represented by Memnon's killing of Antilochus should not blind us to the basic similarities. Nestor may have had his horse wounded by Paris, not

---

[22] The same opinion in, for instance, Rzach 1922:2400.24–25.

his main assailant, and his death may not follow directly upon his son's; but such divergences are hardly impressive, especially when we remember that Vergil's representation of Lausus' end differs so radically from the tradition hitherto current (and preserved for us by Dionysius of Halicarnassus I 65).[23]

Accepted by numerous scholars (e.g. Knauer, *Die Aeneis und Homer: Studien zur poetischen Technik Vergils* [*Hypomnemata* 7 (1964)] 282–283; A. M. Assereto, "Dall' Etiopide all' Eneide," in *Mythos* [Untersteiner Festschrift (Genova 1970)] 54–55), Eduard Fraenkel's thesis has been taken a stage further by G. R. Manton, in "Virgil and the Greek Epic: The Tragedy of Evander," *Journal of the Australasian Universities Language and Literature Association* 17 (1962): 11–13 and 14. As he notes, Evander's speech of farewell to his son Pallas at *Aeneid* VIII 560 reminds us of the Iliadic Nestor (esp. 560 *o ... referat si Iuppiter annos* ∽ *Iliad* VII 132–133: αἲ γάρ, Ζεῦ τε πάτερ καὶ Ἀθηναίη καὶ Ἄπολλον | ἡβῷμ' and cf. *Iliad* VII 157, XI 670–676). But perhaps Vergil's actual model was the Nestor of the *Aethiopis*, and Pallas' fate is colored by Antilochus'. The paradoxical reversal of normality whereby the hero lives long enough into old age to see his son's funeral is endured by both Nestor and Evander: but it is Nestor who is a paradigm for the futility of long life in such circumstances,[24] as represented by Latin poets like Horace *Odes* II 9.13–15, Propertius II 13.49–50, Juvenal X 246–255, and Ausonius *Opuscula* VI 7.4–5. Of the second and third of these passages Allen (in his Oxford text of the Greek Epic Cycle, 127) comments: "*haec ex Arctino, seu recta seu obliqua via, videntur provenisse*," and Manton (16) is more confident and positive that their source was the *Aethiopis*.[25] He also suggests that Vergil's depiction of the death of Turnus at the hands of a vengeful Aeneas is based on the *Aethiopis*'s presentation of the death of Memnon. Manton's views are accepted by Kopff in his examination of Vergil's use of the Epic Cycle (*ANRW* II.31.2:936).

The evidence of art may be able to fill in a detail concerning Nestor's farewell to his son in the *Aethiopis*. Kossatz-Deissmann examined (1981; cf. *LIMC* I.1, *s.v.* "Antilochus," 831–832) fifteen or so red- and black-figure amphoras of the late archaic age which display a remarkably consistent schema, depicting an armed hoplite warrior inspecting, before he departs for battle, a liver held out to him by a παῖς, to the left of whom stands an old man with white beard, ἱμάτιον, and staff. One specimen (a cup by Oltos ca. 510: Vatican [Astarita Coll.]: *ARV*[2] 1623.64 = *LIMC* I.1, *s.v.* "Antilochus," no. 6: see Figure 7) labels the old man as Nestor, thereby allowing us to identify the group as a whole as Antilochus'

[23] See further S. J. Harrison's commentary (Oxford 1991) *ad loc.*
[24] Compare the motif "was it for this that I was allowed to live to this great age?" (examples cited by Ogilvie on Livy II 40.5).
[25] Courteney on Juvenal X 251 says the poet "seems to be thinking of dramatic representations (for *attendas* cf. 6.65) e.g. the *Memnon* of Aeschylus."

Figure 7. "Bilingual" cup, side B: Nestor's farewell to Antilochus (red-figure). Attributed to Oltos, ca. 460 BCE. Museo Gregoriano Etrusco Vaticano, Astarita Collection; formerly AST763, now 35728. Drawing by Valerie Woelfel.

hieroscopy, or more precisely hepatoscopy, before a battle at Troy.[26] Since this practice (on which see the bibliography adduced by Kossatz-Deissmann [1981:567n7] and [specifically on wartime hepatoscopy] W. K. Pritchett, *The Greek State at War* 3 [Berkeley 1979] 74–75) is absent from Homeric epic, Kossatz-Deissmann concludes (567 and 571) that the source for these vases' scene is not an epic, or at least not directly: rather, the schema represents an adjustment, to fit contemporary sixth-century practices, of what was originally an omen of a different type. This latter hypothesis may conceivably be right: such adjustments are not unknown in vase paintings of other scenes from epic (as witness

---

[26] Hardly a battle at Pylos: we would naturally assume that Antilochus was too young to venture out to war in the days before the Trojan expedition, even if Kossatz-Deissmann had not reminded us (1981:570–571) of the tradition found in Philostratus *Heroicus* 3.2, which represents Antilochus as initially too young to join the Greek assault on Troy. He later sneaked into the Greek camp and was saved from his father's anger by Achilles' intervention. For vases which may depict Antilochus' arrival and his father's pacification see Kossatz-Deissmann 1981:570–571 (cf. *LIMC* I.1, 831–832), suggesting a derivation from the *Aethiopis* (the *Cypria* would be another possibility).

those depictions of Priam's visit to Achilles' hut which represent the latter as reclining on a couch while Homer has him seated). Nor would it be difficult to devise an omen which might have stood in the original source: compare the premonitory gloom which surrounds Evander's promise of Pallas' participation in war at Vergil *Aeneid* VIII 521–522 (see P. T. Eden, *A Commentary on the Aeneid: Book VIII* [Leiden 1975] *ad loc.*; on Antilochus as one of the literary models for Pallas see page 62 above).

On the other hand, the way in which the *Aethiopis* exploited the seemingly un-Homeric concept of pollution (pages 56–57 above) should warn us against excessive dogmatism about what religious ideas this lost epic may have utilized, and should deter us from inferring a late entry into Greece of those practices not explicitly attested by Homer. As we have seen, both the *Iliad* and the *Odyssey* present actions which might be interpreted as implying a concept of pollution; likewise both poems, as Kossatz-Deissmann admits (1981:567), mention the figure of the θυοσκόος (*Iliad* XXIV 221; *Odyssey* xxi 145, xxii 318–319).[27]

The link between vase and epic may, in this case, be rather closer than assumed.

καὶ συμβολῆς γενομένης Ἀντίλοχος ὑπὸ Μέμνονος ἀναιρεῖται.
A battle takes place and Antilochus is slain by Memnon.

Tabula Veronensis II: Μέμνων Ἀντίλοχον ἀποκτείνει.

The earliest as well as the fullest extant literary account of the action here occurs in Pindar *Pythian* VI 28–42, where Nestor's son is cited as a paradigm of filial piety:

> ἔγεντο καὶ πρότερον Ἀντίλοχος βιατὰς
> νόημα τοῦτο φέρων,
> ὃς ὑπερέφθιτο πατρός, ἐναρίμβροτον   30
> ἀναμείναις στράταρχον Αἰθιόπων
> Μέμνονα. Νεστόρειον γὰρ ἵππος ἅρμ' ἐπέδα
> Πάριος ἐκ βελέων δαϊχθείς· ὁ δ' ἔφεπεν
> κραταιὸν ἔγχος·
> Μεσσανίου δὲ γέροντος
> δονηθεῖσα φρὴν βόασε παῖδα ὅν·

---

[27] Kossatz-Deissmann's citation (1981:571n27) of "Asclepiades of Myrlea" from Eustathius 1697.52–53 is less reassuring, because the story there quoted, that Antilochus was warned by a certain Chalcon appointed by his father, probably derives from Ptolemaeus Chennus' *New History* (cf. Photius *Bibliotheca* 147.30–32 [2.53–54 Henry]; K.-H. Tomberg, *Die Kaine Historia des Ptolemaios Chennos* [Bonn 1968] 103, 153–154) as argued by Herches, *Fleckeisenii Annales Supplement*, 1.288, followed by B. A. Müller, *De Asclepiade Myrleano* (Leipzig 1903) 17.

χαμαιπετὲς δ' ἄρ' ἔπος οὐκ ἀπέριψεν· αὐτοῦ
μένων δ' ὁ θεῖος ἀνὴρ
πρίατο μὲν θανάτοιο κομιδὰν πατρός,
ἐδόκησέν τε τῶν πάλαι γενεᾶι   40
ὁπλοτέροισιν, ἔργον πελώριον τελέσαις,
ὕπατος ἀμφὶ τοκεῦσιν ἔμμεν πρὸς ἀρετάν.

In view of the numerous later references to the tradition (listed by Willcock [1983:487n7]), the story is unlikely to be a Pindaric invention.

An epic source, specifically the *Aethiopis*, has long been suspected for the lines (so, very early on, Welcker, 2:174), and this particular speculation is followed by various scholars,[28] especially in view of the epic flavor that much of the language seems to possess: with line 32's ἄρμ' ἐπέδα cf. *Iliad* XXIII 585 (δόλωι ἄρμα πεδῆσαι) and with line 37's χαμαιπετὲς ἔπος the Homeric idiom of ἔπεα πτερόεντα. Line 30's ὑπερέφθιτο and ἐναρίμβροτον have an epic feel to them too.

Fraenkel ("Vergil und die Aethiopis," 245–256 = *Kleine Beiträge* 2.176–177) has confirmed the plausibility of the *Aethiopis* as source against the contrary suggestion of Wilamowitz (*Homerische Untersuchungen* [Berlin 1884] 154, 1916:45; see further Fraenkel 245 = 176n2) that the *Ilias Parva* provided Pindar with his inspiration here. Although numerous scholars accepted Wilamowitz's idea (bibliography in Fraenkel 245 = 176n3), it is based on a misunderstanding of *Ilias Parva* F5 (see my note *ad loc.*, in my forthcoming commentary) and may safely be rejected.

ἔπειτα Ἀχιλλεὺς Μέμνονα κτείνει, καὶ τούτωι μὲν Ἠὼς παρὰ Διὸς αἰτη-
σαμένη ἀθανασίαν δίδωσι.
Then Achilles kills Memnon. And the Dawn goddess requests immortality for her son from Zeus and bestows it upon him.

Tabula Veronensis II: Ἀχιλλεὺς Μέμνονα ἀποκτείνει.

---

[28] Christ in his edition ([Leipzig 1846] 185); Gildersleeve *ad loc.* (New York 1885) 318; Kullmann (1960:314); Burton, *Pindar's Pythian Odes* (Oxford 1962) 22; Willcock as cited, etc. Boeckh (*Pindar* II:2.299) actually anticipated Welcker. Some skepticism is expressed by Gruppe, *Gr. Myth.* 1.681n4; and, more recently and radically, A. Kelly ("Neoanalysis and the 'Nestorbedrängnis': A Test Case," *Hermes* 134 [2006]: 13–19). This article argues that Pindar actually bases his narrative on the role of Archilochus in *Iliad* VIII and XXIII, which passages he then undercuts and subverts, often reversing the significance of original motifs to antithetical effect. There is perhaps a method-ological problem about an approach which starts by basing itself on alleged similarities between passages by two authors and ends by stressing the antithetical differences. One might quote against Kelly his (perfectly justified) criticism of a Neo-Neoanalyst (p. 12): "at what point ... do the departures from the proposed model become great enough to sunder the link?"

I have discussed most of the implications of this passage above in connection with the evidence of art and the series of parallels between Achilles and Memnon (pages 31–34). Here it will be enough to refer to J. Th. Kakridis's theory ("Tithonus," *Wiener Studien* 48 [1930]: 36–37) that the present episode's successful plea for immortality is primary in comparison with, and indeed the inspiration of, Eos' bungled attempt at immortality (without everlasting youth) for Memnon's father, Tithonus. We have already seen good cause to doubt the principle that underlies such an approach (page 6 above). Besides, a botched attempt at immortality would seem to be a folk-tale motif in its own right; see my discussion of the contrasting fortunes of Tydeus and his son Diomedes in connection with *Thebais* F5 (*The Theban Epics* [Washington, DC, 2014] 81). In both cases, the hypothesis of a transference of the immortality motif from father to son can by no means be excluded.

Achilles

τρέψαμενος δ' Ἀχιλλεύς τοὺς Τρῶας καὶ εἰς τὴν πόλιν συνεισπεσὼν ὑπὸ Πάριδος ἀναιρεῖται καὶ Ἀπόλλωνος.
Achilles, pursuing the routed Trojans even into the city, is slain by Paris and Apollo.

Tabula Veronensis II: ἐν ταῖς Σκαιαῖς πύλαις Ἀχιλλευ[

Apollodorus *Epitome* 5.3: Ἀχιλλεύς ... πρὸς ταῖς Σκαιαῖς πύλαις τοξεύεται ὑπὸ Ἀλεξάνδρου καὶ Ἀπόλλωνος εἰς τὸ σφυρόν (Achilles is shot at the Scaean Gates by Apollo and Paris, in the heel).

The Scaean Gates are already the witnesses of Achilles' death in *Iliad* XXII 359–360, where Hector's dying and prophetic words warn of the day

ὅτε κέν σε Πάρις καὶ Φοῖβος Ἀπόλλων
ἐσθλὸν ἐόντ' ὀλέσωσιν ἐνὶ Σκαιῇσι πύλῃσιν.

Vian (Budé text of Quintus Smyrnaeus i.169) detects a slight inexactitude of phrasing in Proclus' statement that Achilles had actually entered Troy in pursuit of the fugitive enemy: "en ce cas les Grecs auraient eu beaucoup plus de peine pour ramener la dépouillé d'Achille." Perhaps the statement derives from a misunderstanding of the idiom in a phrase such as ἐν Τροίαι or ἐν πόλει, meaning "at Troy, at the city" (see W. S. Barrett, *Greek Lyric, Tragedy, and Textual Criticism: Collected Papers*, ed. M. L. West [Oxford 2007] 331–332).

At first sight the sources at our disposal seem to differ over the exact responsibility for Achilles' death. Apollo as the sole author is named by Homer (*Iliad* XXI 277–283), Simonides fr.8.11 W, Aeschylus fr. 350 Radt, Sophocles *Philoctetes*

334, Horace *Odes* IV 6.1, and Quintus Smyrnaeus III 60–63; Paris is given responsibility by Euripides *Andromache* 655, *Hecuba* 387, Plutarch *Quaestiones Conviviales* IX 13.2 *Comparison of Lysander and Sulla* 4; the two act together not only in the passages now under scrutiny but at *Iliad* XIX 409–414 and XXII 350–354, and a still more specific account wherein Apollo guides Paris' hand may be found at Vergil *Aeneid* VI 56–58 and Ovid *Metamorphoses* XII 597–606.

As shown by Davies and Finglass on Stesichorus fr. 96, the apparent discrepancies between these three groups are of no great significance and they may all be conveying the same basic information: Apollo inspired and helped Paris to slay Achilles. Even the tradition that Apollo disguised himself as Paris all the better to shoot down his victim (Pindar *Paean* VI 79–80 [cf. Radt *ad loc.* (p. 142)] and Hyginus *Fabulae* 107) need be no more than a further way of symbolizing this. Apollo is shown guiding Paris' arrow against Achilles' heel on a little-published Attic red-figure vase dating to ca. 460 (Bochum, Ruhr-Universität S1060: cf. *LIMC* I.1, *s.v.* "Achilleus," no. 851 = *s.v.* "Alexandros," no. 92). This is, of course, precisely the sort of choice a visual depiction has to make. I still believe, therefore, that Robert's distinction (*Heldensage* 1187; cf. Kakridis 1949:87n40)—which isolates Apollo's guidance of Paris' hand (Vergil and Ovid as cited) as preserving what is actually the earlier tradition—is basically misleading, for all that it has been accepted by numerous scholars (e.g. R. Hampe in Hampe-Simon, *Griechische Sagen in der frühen etruskischen Kunst* [Mainz 1964] 48).

Did the *Aethiopis* also attribute Achilles' death to the one vulnerable part of his body, the famous heel, or has Apollodorus introduced that familiar motif from the later vulgate? Invulnerability is certainly un-Homeric, as Griffin has reminded us (1977:40 = *Oxford Readings in Homer's* Iliad, 368), for it would mitigate and dilute the tragic antithesis of mortals and gods that is so basic to Homer's epics. It would also diminish the heroic valor of his characters. So Antenor can reassure himself without self-deception when awaiting Achilles' onslaught at *Iliad* XXI 568–570:

> καὶ γάρ θην τούτωι, τρωτὸς χρὼς ὀξέϊ χαλχῶι,
> ἐν δὲ ἴα ψυχή, θνητὸν δέ ἕ φασ' ἄνθρωποι
> ἔμμεναι.

Indeed the narrative itself has established Achilles' vulnerability a few hundred lines earlier back in the same book:

> τῶι δ' ἑτέρωι, μιν πῆχυν ἐπιγράβδην βάλε χειρὸς
> δεξιτερῆς, σύτο δ' αἷμα κελαινεφές.
>
> XXI 166–167

If Homer, in a manner that can be paralleled elsewhere, has excluded Achilles' invulnerability from his epic world, the *Aethiopis* would not be uncharacteristic of later epic if it restored this detail. The alternative explanation of the facts—that Achilles' invulnerability was actually unknown to Homer because it was a late, a very late, invention—receives its most extreme and eloquent exposition from Otto Berthold, *Die Unverwundbarkeit in Sage und Aberglauben der Griechen* (*Religionsgeschichtliche Versuche und Vorarbeiten* 11 [1911]) 35, a work cited with glowing approval by Bethe (1922:231n1). Berthold would reckon the majority of Greek legends about unwoundable heroes to be of late origin, not least the most famous and well-known case of Thetis' son. It must be said that few of his arguments convince. In particular, the idea that the multiplicity of arrows implied by such phrases as Ἀπόλλωνος βελέεσσιν[29] (*Iliad* XXI 277) or ἐν πολέμωι τόξοις ἀπὸ ψυχὰν λιπών (Pindar *Pythian* III 100) rules out vulnerability in one isolated part of the body (Berthold 36–37) is to be rejected out of hand. The plurals may be poetic, as Berthold himself allows. Words referring to tools or weapons often take a plural, signifying their compound nature (especially τόξον, where the plural usually signifies "bow with arrows": see e.g. Moorhouse, *The Syntax of Sophocles* [*Mnemosyne* Suppl. 75 (1982)] 4–5).

Furthermore, Berthold's claim (37–38) that the motif of invulnerability has been transferred to Achilles from his armor, which was originally (though, again, not in the *Iliad*) conceived of as impenetrable (cf. Griffin 1977:40 = *Oxford Readings in Homer's* Iliad, 368; Ph. J. Kakridis, "Achilles' Rustung," *Hermes* 89 [1961]: 288–297) has very little to recommend it. The exact reverse may have been the case, as is argued by (for instance) E. Drerup, *Das Homerproblem in der Gegenwart: Prinzipien und Methoden der Homererklärung* (Würzburg 1921) 231n3. Even Berthold considers this possibility seriously, but rejects it because he can find no convincing evidence for the early existence of the hero's invulnerability from which the weapon's magic powers might derive. On the possibility that impenetrable armor and skin amount to the same thing, see Davies, "The Hero and His Arms" (as cited above, page 60), 154.

The strongest argument at Berthold's disposal is that *ex silentio*. Not so much the absence of any explicit literary reference[30] before the staggeringly late testimony of Statius *Achilleid* I 269–270 (*si progenitum Stygos amne severo | armavi*) et al. (see Berthold 35), but the lack of any allusion to Achilles' invulnerability in the

---

[29] The plural is taken literally by Pestalozzi (1945:17), followed by Hampe in Hampe-Simon, *Griechische Sagen in der frühen etruskischen Kunst*, 49, who refers it to the version of the *Aethiopis* and the Chalcidian vase considered on the next page.

[30] Some take Paris' wounding of Diomedes with an arrow in the foot (*Iliad* XI 369–377) to reflect the scene in the *Aethiopis* where Achilles is killed (see, for instance, Andersen, *Die Diomedesgestalt in der Ilias* (*Symbolae Osloenses* Suppl. 25 [1978]) 10). Note the warning of Fenik (*Iliad X and the Rhesus: The Myth* [*Collection Latomus* 73 (1964)] 95–96) on the Iliadic scene's typical elements.

Figure 8. Chalcidian black-figure amphora: the corpse of Achilles lies on the battlfield, his left ankle pierced by an arrow. Ca. 6th century BCE. Vase is now lost; drawing after R. Hampe and E. Simon, *Griechische Sagen in der frühen etruskischen Kunst* (Mainz 1964), Abb. 10.

Iliadic scholia (contrast the relative profusion of their comments upon Ajax's very human capacity for wounds in their poem: see pages 84–85 below) and Achilles' failure to figure along with Caeneus, Cycnus, and Ajax in the fourth-century A.D. Palaephatus' περὶ ἀπίστων as another invulnerable hero (Festa, *Mythographi Graeci* 3.2 [Leipzig 1902]) are both disturbing. Berthold may further be right to insist (38) that the silence is not mitigated to any significant degree by the alternative tradition of Thetis' foiled attempt to achieve immortalization of Achilles by fire. True, this version is found in authors who, if not early in an absolute sense, are at least far earlier than the time of Domitian: Apollonius of Rhodes IV 869–879 is the first of them. But Berthold argues that invulnerability did not originally feature in the tradition here and it seems impossible to disprove him (see Richardson's commentary on the *Homeric Hymn to Demeter* pp. 231–232 for a full discussion of the numerous interpretations that have been placed upon this and similar legends). It may be (so Berthold 42) an altogether later importation meant to explain the equally late invulnerability tradition.

Nevertheless, this argument is not overwhelming: if early literature seems strangely silent, early art is not so mute, unless we deliberately shut our ears to its information. A famous Chalcidian vase of the sixth century, no longer (alas) with us (*LIMC* I.1, *s.v.* "Achilleus," no. 850: see Figure 8), showed a busy mêlée surrounding the corpse of Achilles. This active throng we will examine later (see page 71 below). What concerns us here is that from the left ankle of this corpse—raised, as a Trojan tries to drag it by the attached thong—three gouts of blood were dripping. Which is hardly surprising, because that ankle had been quite transfixed by an arrow from the bow of the nearby Paris. It is true that an equal amount of blood is oozing from a second wound located in the corpse's trunk[31]—but this hardly alters the main point.

If Hampe (48) is right to suppose, as do most scholars,[32] that the vase's picture is "in engem Anschluss an die *Aithiopis*," can we not deduce that this epic represented Achilles as vulnerable only in one heel? And is not this deduction reinforced by the red-figure vase cited above (page 67), which shows Apollo and Paris aiming at Achilles' heel?

Berthold insists (36) that the concept of a wound in the heel—found also in Apollodorus *Epitome* 5.3: ὁ Ἀχιλλεύς ... πρὸς ταῖς Σκαιαῖς πύλαις τοξεύεται εἰς τὸ σφυρόν—does not necessarily imply that Achilles was invulnerable in all other parts of his body. This is surely preposterous. Even if one accepts[33] his assurance that mythical heroes the world over are capable of succumbing to a trivial wound in the foot (36n1), it would be an intolerable coincidence that an early tradition of an Achilles wounded in the heel should have first originated and then existed for so long a time without any connection at all with the story of Thetis and the Styx. Are we really wrong to see the latter as presupposed by the former? The freak that arises if we are thus mistaken seems to me a close relative of that other freak which comes into being when we refuse to identify the apple carried by one of the three goddesses on vase paintings of the Judgment of Paris with the prize for beauty specifically attested only in later sources.

This conclusion is supported by examination of the analogous stories of invulnerability that occur throughout the world. Berthold himself mentions several of those (especially from Germany), and there is a useful bibliography of various collections of relevant material in Stith Thompson's *Motif Index* 5.Z311 s.v. "Invulnerability except in one spot." See further K. Ranke in *Enzyklopädie des Märchens*, 1.59, s.v. "Achillesferse"; M. L. West, *Indo-European Poetry and Myth* (Oxford 2007) 444–446; and P. Thordarson, "Die Ferse des Achilleus: Ein Skythisches Motiv?," *Symbolae Osloenses* 47 (1972): 109–124, especially 112–115. These establish beyond doubt the primitive and widespread nature of the theme.

An invulnerable Ajax may have featured in the *Aethiopis* (see page 84 below). The motif was certainly used of him by the time of Aeschylus' Θρῇσσαι (see page 86 below). Did the ancient world really have to wait until Statius before

---

[31] F. Jouan ("Le Cycle épique: État des questions," in *Association Guillaume Budé, Actes du Xe Congrès* [Paris 1980] 94) confidently assumes that one arrow derives from Apollo, the other from Paris (but see page 67 above).

[32] See, for instance, Robert, *Heldensage* 2.1188n5; *LIMC* I.1 183.

[33] And one should probably not, because one of his examples, the Celtic hero Diarmaid, is pricked in the heel by the *poisonous* bristle of a boar, while he is measuring its hide by walking over it. Besides, as the late but still lamented Edwin Ardener once informed me, this particular version of the legend is so late that contamination from the tradition of Achilles' heel cannot be ruled out.

its application to the greater hero occurred to someone?[34] The little-known Hellenistic gold ring (Los Angeles County Museum of Art 61.48.2: *LIMC* I.1, *s.v.* "Achilleus," no. 12) which shows Thetis dipping her son in the Styx finally removes[35] that question from the world of rhetoric.

καὶ περὶ τοῦ πτώματος[36] γενομένης ἰσχυρᾶς μάχης Αἴας ἀνελόμενος ἐπὶ τὰς ναῦς κομίζει, Ὀδυσσέως ἀπομαχομένου τοῖς Τρῶσιν.

And over the dead Achilles a mighty battle arises, during which Ajax takes up and carries the corpse to the ships, while Odysseus fights a rearguard battle against the Trojans.

> Apollodorus *Epitome* 5.4: γενομένης δὲ μάχης περὶ τοῦ νεκροῦ, Αἴας Γλαῦκον ἀναιρεῖ, καὶ τὰ ὅπλα δίδωσιν ἐπὶ τὰς ναῦς κομίζειν, τὸ δὲ σῶμα βαστάσας Αἴας βαλλόμενος βέλεσι μέσον τῶν πολεμίων διήνεγκεν, Ὀδυσσέως πρὸς τοὺς ἐπιφερομένους μαχομένου (A battle arises over [Achilles'] corpse. Ajax slays Glaucus and gives the weapons [of Achilles] to carry to the ships, and, supporting the corpse, transports it through the midst of the enemy, being pelted with missiles all the while. Odysseus fights off [Trojans] trying to charge).

Wagner (*Curae Mythographicae* 210–211) supposes that here—as often elsewhere—Apollodorus can be used to supplement a Proclean résumé that in this case becomes so summary at one particular point as to give the wrong impression. The additional details thus supplied concern the following two issues.

(i) Ajax and Glaucus

Ajax's killing of Glaucus recurs in Quintus Smyrnaeus III 243–266 (see also VIII 105, XIV 135–136), Hyginus *Fabulae* 113 (without context in a list entitled *nobilem quem quis occidit*), and on the labeled Chalcidian vase (no longer extant) that we mentioned above (page 69).[37] Here Ajax bestraddles Achilles' corpse and runs his spear through Glaucus, who has fastened a noose to Achilles' pierced heel in order to drag him back to the Trojan ranks (compare Hippothous' similar

---

[34] In book I of his *Posthomerica* Quintus of Smyrna stresses the association between Achilles and Ajax: for details see Vian's Budé text of that poet i.9. Vian suggests that this association (pointless in Quintus' narrative, where Ajax retires before the decisive battle) derives from our epic, where it would have given a sort of unity, since the main climaxes of the poem were the deaths of the two heroes.

[35] Robert, *Heldensage* 67 supposed the dipping to be a Hellenistic invention.

[36] σώματος was conjectured by Schubart (*Ephemerides Literariae Helmstadienses* 1 [1840] 517), but Wagner (*Curae Mythographicae de Apollodori fontibus* [Leipzig 1891] 209n2) observed that πτῶμα "apud recentiores scriptores" could refer to a "cadaver humi prostratum" and cited Polybius XV 14.2. Note in particular the πτῶμα Ἀχιλλέως mentioned in *Ilias Parva* fr. 2ᵇ.

[37] Bibliography in Rzach 1922:2402.57; Jouan, "Le Cycle épique: État des questions," in *Association Guillaume Budé, Actes du Xᵉ Congrès* (Paris 1980) 94n37.

attempt [at *Iliad* XVII 289][38] to gain the corpse of Patroclus). Athena lends Ajax some much-needed support, brandishing her spear behind him. Ajax's shield is already laden with enemy spears and at least one arrow. Paris is aiming another at him and behind Paris loom Aeneas (cf. Quintus of Smyrna III 278–286) and a further warrior, Laodocus (cf. *Iliad* IV 87), their spears at the ready. The depiction of Diomedes, wounded in the wrist and standing apart, could, as Robert (*Heldensage* 2.1185n5) observes, be a free rendering of *Iliad* V 95–100 (that hero wounded in the shoulder) or an attempt (by the artist or by the poet of the *Aethiopis*: Severyns 1928:322) to explain Diomedes' failure to figure more prominently in the rescue of and dispute the subject of our next issue.

(ii) The Arms of Achilles

The arms of Achilles are separately sent on ahead to the ships while his corpse is fought over. This separation of the armor from the corpse has an analogy of sorts in *Iliad* XVII 125–127, where, in spite of the earlier statement (at *Iliad* XVI 791–796) to the effect that Apollo had struck off the helmet, shield, and breastplate from his helpless victim, Hector is now described as stripping the dead Patroclus of his armor and then retreating before the advance of Ajax. He hands over the armor to fellow Trojans for them to carry it back to Troy; but after the scene outlined above he catches them up and dons the armor himself (189–192). Achilles' corpse is regularly depicted naked (cf. *LIMC* I.1, *s.v.* "Achilleus," no. 192) in art.

In literature, of course, Achilles' armor must be saved in order to be quarreled over by Ajax and Odysseus, and similarly the division of responsibilities between the two in rescuing the corpse must be such as to give each a plausible claim when the contest arises. In the rescuing of Patroclus' body at *Iliad* XVII 715–736, Ajax seems to bear the brunt (and the honors).[39] Contrast *Odyssey* v 309–310:

ὅτε μοι πλεῖστοι χαλκήρεα δοῦρα
Τρῶες ἐπέρριψαν περὶ Πηλείωνι θανόντι.

Σ BPQ *ad loc.* claim that Odysseus took charge of the body while Ajax came up behind. Now this seems the less likely to be a misremembering of *Iliad* XVII 716–721 or the general Iliadic picture of Ajax as the hero of defense in view of

---

[38] Gruppe (*Gr. Myth* 1.682n5) supposed this portion of the *Iliad* to derive from the *Aethiopis* because of the similarity between Homer's narrative and the contents of this vase. E. Howald, *Der Mythos als Dichtung* (Zurich 1946) 31–32 also finds the Iliadic passage a "Nachahmung" of the rescue of Achilles' body.

[39] The views of Aristarchus (as preserved in Σ A *Iliad* XVII 719 [4.426 Erbse: to the discussions he cites *ad loc.* add Severyns 1928:321–322]: see van Thiel 2014:3.150) were that to carry Achilles' corpse was not a task for Ajax, and that Homer would have made no such oversight, unlike οἱ νεώτεροι.

the publication of a fragment of epic (*P.Oxy.* 2510) in which Odysseus proposes to carry the corpse (line 13) and then actually raises it (line 21). Cf. West, "New Fragments of Greek Poetry," *Classical Review* 16 (1966): 22; F. Jouan, "Le Cycle épique: État des questions," in *Association Guillaume Budé, Actes du Xe Congrès* (Paris 1980) 86 and n10 on the work's date.

But in deciding whether other authors subscribe to this version, one must look out for tendentiousness. The essentially negative nature of Odysseus' rôle, for instance, is masterfully transformed into something much more positive and heroic in those passages where ancient authors place Odysseus on the defense (e.g. Sophocles *Philoctetes* 372–373: ναί, παῖ, δεδώκασ' ἐνδίκως οὗτοι τάδε· | ἐγὼ γὰρ αὖτ' ἔσωσα; Ovid *Metamorphoses* XIII 284–285: *his ... humeris ego corpus Achillis | et simul arma tuli*).[40] Crudely malicious diminution of Odysseus' activity replaces distortion with the opposite bent at Quintus Smyrnaeus V 219–222 when Ajax in his claim to Achilles' armor quite omits his rival's part in the action:

> ὅτ' ἀμφ' Ἀχιλῆι δεδουπότι δῆρις ὀρώρει,
> ὄφρ' ἐκ δυσμενέων με καὶ ἀργαλέοιο κυδοιμοῦ
> ἔδρακες ἔντεα καλὰ ποτὶ κλισίας φορέοντα
> αὐτῶι ὁμῶς Ἀχιλῆι δαΐφρονι.

Depictions in art likewise elevate Ajax's and ignore Odysseus' rôle, as E. Kunze, *Archaische Schildbänder: Ein Beitrag zur frühgriechischen Bildgeschichte und Sagen-überlieferung* (*Olympische Forschungen* 2 [1950]) 151–152 rightly stresses. One might cite, for instance, Odysseus' absence from the Chalcidian vase described above (page 69).[41]

Severyns (1928:322) supposes that our epic's depiction of Achilles' death "n'était point sans beauté ni sans grandeur" and adds that its presentation of the struggle over Achilles' corpse is "la partie qui devait être la plus belle et la plus émouvante de l'*Éthiopide*" (320). One would certainly like to think so.

καὶ Θέτις ἀφικομένη σὺν Μούσαις καὶ ταῖς ἀδελφαῖς θρηνεῖ τὸν παῖδα.
Thetis arrives with the Muses and her sisters [the Nereids] and laments over her son.

The Capitoline Tabula Iliaca (see page 98 below) shows Thetis and a single Muse at an altar to which they may be bringing offerings. A further incompletely

---

[40] Cf. Antisthenes' *Ajax* (*Artium scriptores* B 19.11.12 Radermacher) and R. Pfeiffer, *History of Classical Scholarship: From the Beginnings to the End of the Hellenistic Age* (Oxford 1968) 1.36–37 and 37n2.

[41] A. Schneider, *Der troische Sagenkreis in der ältesten griechische Kunst* (Leipzig 1886) 157, followed by Rzach (1922:2403.13–20), argued that the vase showed the battle before Odysseus' arrival on the scene. But this explanation will not do since Odysseus is also omitted from depictions of the transportation of the corpse back to the Greek camp (on these see *LIMC* I.1, s.v. "Achilleus," 185–192).

preserved female figure at the right may represent a Nereid. It is likely that the fallen body visible behind the Muse is meant as Achilles. A similar account of events leading up to Achilles' funeral is contained within the notorious "Second Νέκυια."

At *Odyssey* xxiv 42–97 Agamemnon finds it mysteriously appropriate to enlighten Achilles as to events ten years past. After his death in battle the latter was placed on a pyre and washed and anointed. The Greeks wept over him and cut their tresses. And then (47–49)

> μήτηρ δ' ἐξ ἁλὸς ἦλθε σὺν ἀθανάτῃς ἁλίῃσιν
> ἀγγελίης ἀΐουσα· βοή δ' ἐπί πόντον ὀρώρει
> θεσπεσίῃ, ὑπό δὲ τρόμος ἔλλαβε πάντας Ἀχαίους.

The nature and source of line 48's ἀγγελίη is a great mystery, but the ἀθάναται ἁλίαι mentioned in xxiv 47 and 55 are clearly Thetis' sisters the Nereids, the κοῦραι ἁλίοιο γέροντος of line 58.

A well-timed speech from Nestor (51–56) checks the panic referred to above. After this (58–61):

> ἀμφὶ δέ σ' ἔστησαν κοῦραι ἁλίοιο γέροντος
> οἴκτρ' ὀλοφυρόμεναι, περί δ' ἄμβροτα εἵματα ἔσσαν,
> Μοῦσαι δ' ἐννέα πᾶσαι ἀμειβόμεναι ὀπί καλῇι
> θρήνεον.

The similarity cannot be denied: how is it to be explained? Are the Odyssean lines indebted to the *Aethiopis* (so, for instance P. Von der Mühll, *RE* 7 [1940]: 765.16 = *Ausgewählte kleine Schriften* [Basel 1975] 117) or vice versa (F. Blass, *Die Interpolationen in der Odyssee* [Berlin 1904] 285)?

Dihle (1970:17)[42] argues that the *Aethiopis* cannot be the source, because in that poem Achilles was granted immortality, whereas in *Odyssey* xxiv he is very much a ghost, a spirit conversing with other spirits in Hades.

As commentators (e.g. Ameis–Hentze–Cauer *ad loc.*) observe, the passages in *Odyssey* and *Aethiopis* recall the lamentation in *Iliad* XXIV 718–776, with the Muses taking the role of the *Iliad*'s ἀοιδοί who are θρήνων ἔξαρχοι (720–721). Thetis' sisters, as kinswomen of Achilles, occupy the position of Andromache, Hecuba, and Helen, who are contrasted with the singers at line 722:

> οἱ μὲν δὴ θρήνεον, ἐπί σε στενάχοντο γυναῖκες.

For a detailed account of the mechanics of such a θρῆνος, see M. Alexiou, *The Ritual Lament in Greek Tradition* (Cambridge 1974). Note the evidence of Philostratus *On*

---

[42] Followed by H. Erbse, *Beiträge zum Verständnis der Odyssee* (Berlin 1972) 194n72.

Heroes 51.7 (p. 65 de Lannoy): ἀποθανόντα Ἀχιλλέα Μοῦσαι μὲν ὠιδαῖς ἐθρή-νησαν, Νηρηΐδες δὲ πληγαῖς τῶν στέρνων.

The Muses' lament over Achilles' body is glancingly mentioned by Pindar *Isthmian* VIII 57–58:

> ἀλλά οἱ παρά τε πυρὰν τάφον θ' Ἑλικώνιαι παρθένοι
> στάν, ἐπὶ θρῆνόν τε πολύφαμον ἔχεαν.

From Quintus Smyrnaeus III 594 and Tzetzes *Posthomerica* 435 we learn the unsurprising news that they arrived from Helicon. That goddesses like the Muses should come to lament over a mortal, even if that mortal be Achilles, is very striking, especially when we remember the usual reluctance of most Greek deities to witness death. (See Barrett on Euripides *Hippolytus* 1437, esp. the anecdote cited from Aelian fr. 11 in which the Muses quit the house of a dying poet.)

A Muse appears at the end of the *Rhesus* and tells the dead hero (977) θρήνοις ἀδελφαὶ πρῶτα μὲν σὲ ὑμνήσομεν, but she constitutes a special case because she is Rhesus' mother. Different again is the point made at Euripides *Trojan Women* 511: ἀμφί μοι Ἴλιον, ὦ | Μοῦσα, καινῶν ὕμνων | ἄεισον ἐν δακρύοις ὠιδὰν ἐπικήδειον, and in an Attic Scolion (see page 77 below), 880 *PMG* (of Linus: Μοῦσαι δέ σε θρηνέουσιν), and Naevius fr. 64.1–2 (p. 69 Blänsdorf): *inmortales mortales si foret fas flere, | flerent divae Camenae Naevium poetam.* Since the Muses appeared at the wedding of Peleus and Thetis (so Proclus' summary of the *Cypria*) it may have been thought appropriate that they should mourn the death of that union's offspring. Both features seem alien to the Homeric poems, where the barriers between mortal and divine are scrupulously observed.

On Thetis' mourning for Achilles in later writers see F. Williams, *Callimachus' Hymn to Apollo* (Oxford 1978) 31. On Nereids as mourners see A. Nock, *Essays on Religion and the Ancient World* (Oxford 1972) 2:925, J. M. Barringer, *Divine Escorts: Nereids in Archaic and Classical Greek Art* (Michigan 1995) 49–58.

Both Lament and Funeral Games are closely connected as ways of honoring the dead (cf. K. Meuli, *Der griechische Agon: Kampf und Kampfspiel im Totenbrauch, Totentanz, Totenklage und Totenlob* [Cologne 1968] 82), and it is interesting to see that the latter followed the former in the *Aethiopis*.

Severyns, who had a touching admiration for this totally vanished poem, assures us that the epic's treatment of Achilles' funeral must have displayed "une grandeur et une émotion" (1928:322).

καὶ τὸν νεκρὸν τοῦ Ἀχιλλέως προτίθενται.
And they lay out the corpse of Achilles.

For the verb with this meaning see LSJ *s.v.* προτίθημι II.1. On the mechanics and significance of the whole ritual see the indexes *s.v.* "prothesis" in Kurtz–Boardman,

Greek Burial Customs (London 1971) and Alexiou; on the archaeological evidence see also G. Ahlberg, *Prothesis and Ekphora in Greek Geometric Art* (Göteborg 1971). Cf. Burkert, *Griechische Religion der archaischen und klassischen Epoche* (Stuttgart 1977) 295–296 = 192 (Engl. transl.).

καὶ μετὰ ταῦτα ἐκ τῆς πυρᾶς ἡ Θέτις ἀναρπάσασα τὸν παῖδα εἰς τὴν
Λευκὴν νῆσον διακομίζει.
And after this Thetis snatches up her son from the funeral pyre and carries him across to the island of Leuce,

Robert (*Heldensage*, 1194) assumes that here Thetis snatched up from the pyre "das unsterbliche Teil ihres Sohnes." Cf. T. C. W. Stinton, *Journal of Hellenic Studies* Suppl. 15 (1987) 1–3 = *Collected Papers on Greek Tragedy* (Oxford 1990) 493–495. Compare the apotheosis of Heracles through the burning of his mortal part (cf. Richardson on *Homeric Hymn to Demeter* 231–255 [pp. 231–236]). Leuce is briefly alluded to by Euripides *Andromache* 1260–1262 (Thetis to Peleus): τὸν φίλτατον σοὶ παῖδ' ἐμοί τ' Ἀχιλλέα | ὄψηι δόμους ναίοντα νησιωτικοὺς | Λευκὴν κατ' ἀκτὴν ἐντὸς ἀξένου πόρου. Compare too his *Iphigenia in Tauris* 435–438 (τὰν πολυόρνιθον ἐπ' αἶαν, λευκὰν ἀκτάν, Ἀχιλῆος δρόμους καλλισταδίους, | ἄξεινον κατὰ πόντον) and Pindar *Nemean* IV 49–50 (ἐν δ' Εὐξείνωι πελάγει φαεννὰν Ἀχιλεὺς | νᾶσον [ἔχει]). For other sources see West 2013:156n43.

On the wider tradition of Achilles' immortality see H. Hommel, *Der Gott Achilleus* (*Sitzungsberichte der Heidelberger Akademie der Wissenschaften Philosophisch-historische Klasse* [1980]); J. Burgess, *The Death and Afterlife of Achilles* (Baltimore 2009); West, *Indo-European Poetry and Myth* (Oxford 2007) 349. The *Aethiopis* is the earliest attested reference to this tradition and its localization at Leuce. On the significance of our passage see especially the comments of Rohde (1886.1:87 = 65 [Engl. transl.]): "the author of the *Aethiopis*—always remarkable for his bold innovations in the traditional material—here ventures upon an important new touch." That Thetis restored Achilles to life on Leuce, he proceeds,

> and made him immortal the one meagre extract … does not say. But
> there can be no question that that is what the poet narrated—all later
> accounts conclude the story in this way. The parallel is clear: the two
> opponents, Achilles and Memnon, are both set free from the fate of
> mortals by their goddess-mothers. In bodies once more restored to life
> they continue to live, not among men, nor yet among the gods, but
> in a distant wonderland—Memnon in the East, Achilles in the "White
> Island." The poet himself can hardly have imagined Achilles' Island
> to have been in the Euxine Sea, where, however, later Greek sailors
> located this purely mythical spot.

On Leuce and Achilles' connection with it see further Rohde 1886:371n2 = 565n101, and Hommel, *Der Gott Achilleus*, index *s.v.* "Leuke (Insel)," Burgess Index *s.v.* Some sort of cult to Achilles on the island is clearly presupposed, and the activities of Milesian colonists in the area of the Black Sea may well (*pace* Rohde) be a relevant datum when we are considering the interpretation of a poem attributed to the Milesian Arctinus. See further G. Hedreen, "The Cult of Achilles in the Euxine," *Hesperia* 60 (1991): 313–330, J. Hupe (ed.), *Der Achilleus-Kult im nördlichen Schwarzmeerraum* (Rahden 2006).

An alternative (though equally favorable) fate awaits Achilles in those authors who have the hero transported to the Islands of the Blessed, where he dwells among other worthies:

> Πηλεύς τε καὶ Κάδμος ἐν τοῖσιν ἀλέγονται·
> Ἀχιλλέα τ' ἔνεικ', ἐπεὶ Ζηνὸς ἦτορ
> λιταῖς ἔπεισε, μάτηρ·
> ὃς Ἕκτορα σφᾶλε, Τροίας
> ἄμαχον ἀστραβῆ κίονα, Κύκνον τε θανάτωι πόρεν,
> Ἀοῦς τε παῖδ' Αἰθιόπα.
>
> Pindar Olympian II 78–83

> φίλταθ' Ἁρμόδι', οὔ τί πω τέθνηκας
> νήσοις δ' ἐν μακάρων σέ φασιν εἶναι,
> ἵνα περ ποδώκης Ἀχιλεύς.
>
> Carmen Conviviale 849.1–3 PMG

> ὥσπερ Ἀχιλλέα τὸν τῆς Θέτιδος υἱὸν ἐτίμησαν καὶ εἰς μακάρων νήσους ἀπέπεμψαν.
>
> Plato Symposium 179ᵉ

or to the Elysian Plain:

> ὅτι δὲ Ἀχιλλεὺς εἰς τὸ Ἡλύσιον πεδίον παραγενόμενος ἔγημε Μήδειαν πρῶτος Ἴβυκος [fr. 291 *PMGF*] εἴρηκε, μεθ' ὃν Σιμωνίδης [fr. 558 P].
>
> Σ Apollonius of Rhodes IV 814–815 (p. 293 Wendel)

On the μακάρων νῆσοι: see Rohde (above) and West on Hesiod *Works and Days* 171. A passage such as *Odyssey* iv 561–568 reminds us how similar the Elysian Plain was to these. See further Hommel, *Der Gott Achilleus*, 18–22 and F. Solmsen, "Achilles on the Islands of the Blessed: Pindar vs. Homer and Hesiod," *American Journal of Philology* 103 (1982): 19.

For the variant whereby Helen becomes Achilles' wife on Leuce (first attested in Pausanias III 19.13) see Hommel, *Der Gott Achilleus*, 27.

οἱ δὲ Ἀχαιοὶ τὸν τάφον χώσαντες ἀγῶνα τιθέασι.
And the Greeks pile up Achilles' funeral mound and carry out the rites.

On the grave mound here erected for Achilles in spite of his body's translation to Leuce see Rohde 1886.1:87–88n2 = 94n29 (Engl. transl.). He explains it in terms of "a concession to the older narrative (*Odyssey* xxiv 80–84) which knew nothing of the translation of the body but gives prominence to the grave-mound. Besides which, the tumulus of Achilles—a landmark on the seashore of the Troad—required explanation." Rhode cites other examples of cenotaphs to "translated" heroes. Compare Davies and Finglass on Stesichorus fr. 178.

Funeral games were a common focus of heroic activity and poetry for the ancients: they are often mentioned in the *Iliad* (cf. *Iliad* XI 699). XXII 162–897 τὰ ἄθλα ἐπὶ Πατρόκλωι in *Iliad* XXIII are perhaps the most famous (see Willcock 1973) and even within these we find references to the further funeral games of Amarynceus (630–643) and Oedipus (679).

Outside Homer the ἄθλα ἐπὶ Πελίαι were particularly popular: see Davies and Finglass, *Stesichorus: The Poems* 212 and in general L. Malten, "Leichenspiel und Totenkult," *Mitteilungen des Deutschen Archäologischen Instituts, Römische Abteilung* 38–39 (1923–1924): 300; K. Meuli, *Der griechische Agon: Kampf und Kampfspiel im Totenbrauch, Totentanz, Totenklage und Totenlob* (Cologne 1968) 15.

The present funeral games are briefly outlined by Agamemnon to Achilles in *Odyssey* xxiv 85–92 (see page 74 above):

> μήτηρ δ' αἰτήσασα θεοὺς περικαλλέ' ἄεθλα   85
> θῆκε μέσωι ἐν ἀγῶνι ἀριστήεσσιν Ἀχαιῶν.
> ἤδη μὲν πολέων τάφωι ἀνδρῶν ἀντεβόλησας
> ἡρώων, ὅτε κέν ποτ' ἀποφθιμένου βασιλῆος
> ζώννυνταί τε νέοι. καὶ ἐπεντύνονται ἄεθλα·
> ἀλλά κε κεῖνα μάλιστα ἰδὼν θηήσαο θυμῶι,   90
> οἵ' ἐπὶ σοὶ κατέθηκε θεὰ περικαλλέ' ἄεθλα,
> ἀργυρόπεζα Θέτις· μάλα γὰρ φίλος ἦσθα θεοῖσιν.

This tells us little more than that the prizes were fetched by Thetis from the gods, rather like Achilles' own weapons. Apollodorus *Epitome* 5.5 adds that the chariot race was won by Eumelus, the foot race by Diomedes, the discus throwing by Ajax, and the archery contest by Teucer. These details too may go back to the *Aethiopis*, as suggested, for instance, by Vian, Budé text of Quintus Smyrnaeus i.134. Robert (*Heldensage* 1189n1) observes the general resemblance between

Apollodorus' list of events and victors and the Funeral Games for Patroclus in *Iliad* XXIII,[43] where, however, Diomedes unexpectedly wins the chariot race in keeping with his importance for the themes of the whole poem (see Andersen 1978:142–144) and, just as unexpectedly, Meriones defeats Teucer in the archery contest. Whether Thetis played any role (cf. *Odyssey* xxiv 92) in the *Aethiopis'* games is unclear.[44]

καὶ περὶ τῶν Ἀχιλλέως ὅπλων Ὀδυσσεῖ καὶ Αἴαντι στάσις ἐμπίπτει.
And a quarrel arises between Odysseus and Ajax over the arms of Achilles.

> Apollodorus *Epitome* 5.5: τὴν δὲ Ἀχιλλέως πανοπλίαν τῶι ἀρίστωι νικητήριον τιθεῖσι, καὶ καταβαίνουσιν εἰς ἅμιλλαν Αἴας καὶ Ὀδυσσεὺς καὶ κρινάντων τῶν Τρώων ... Ὀδυσσεὺς προκρίνεται (The armor of Achilles is selected as victory prize for the best hero. Ajax and Odysseus enter the contest and, with the Trojans acting as judges, ... Odysseus is deemed the winner).

From our point of view there are three versions as to how a decision was reached. According to one, Nestor prompted the Greeks to send spies to the walls of Troy, where they overheard two girls debating the relative merits of Ajax and Odysseus. Since this tradition is explicitly assigned to the *Ilias Parva* (F2), I shall discuss it in my commentary *ad loc.* A second version had the Greeks themselves draw up a panel of judges who voted in favor of Odysseus. Compare Pindar *Nemean* VIII 26–27 (κρυφίαισι γὰρ ἐν ψάφοις Ὀδυσσῆ Δαναοὶ θεράπευσαν· | χρυσέων δ' Αἴας στερηθεὶς ὅπλων φόνωι πάλαισεν) and Sophocles *Ajax* 1135 (Teucer upbraids Menelaus): Τεῦκρος – κλέπτης γὰρ αὐτοῦ ψηφοποιὸς ηὑρέθης. | Μενέλαος – ἐν τοῖς δικασταῖς, κοὐκ ἐμοί, τόδ' ἐσφάλη. | Τεῦκρος – πόλλ' ἂν κακῶς λάθραι σὺ κλέψειας κακά.[45] This account underlies the scenes of the

---

[43] According to Kullmann (1960:112), "der tatsächliche Sieg [of Eumelus] in der *Aithiopis* erscheint—rein stofflich—gegenüber der blossen Erwartung des Sieges in der *Ilias* primär."

[44] Thetis also features as arranger of the games at Quintus Smyrnaeus IV 103–104. Vian *ad loc.* (i.140n3) distinguishes this from the *Aethiopis*'s version, where Thetis seems to be absent, having removed her son's corpse to Leuce, and the Achaeans are specified as the organizers. But Proclus' summary is too brief for us to be absolutely certain that she may not have returned in our epic to supervise the funerary tributes to her son.

[45] For later literary allusions to this version see Vian, Budé text of Quintus Smyrnaeus ii.8n1 (he includes Apollodorus *Epitome* 5.6 [καὶ κρινάντων τῶν Τρώων, ὡς δέ τινες τῶν συμμάχων, Ὀδυσσεὺς προκρίνεται], where, however, the σύμμαχοι are surely the Trojan allies [as supposed by Noack, review of F. Kehmptzow, *De Quinti Smyrnaei fontibus ac mythopoeia*, in *Göttingische Gelehrte Anzeiger* (1892): 780n4: cf. Apollodorus *Epitome* 3.34, 4.4, etc.; *contra* Gruppe, *Gr. Myth.* 1.683n4) and the detail an odd autoschediasm. The implications of fraud in the voting which we encounter in the two earliest extant testimonia (on κρυφίος in the Pindaric passage as entailing crooked, not secret, votes see N. O. Brown, "Pindar, Sophocles, and the Thirty Years Peace," *Transactions*

Greek chieftains voting under the watchful eyes of Athena which we find on a famous cup by Douris (Vienna 3695: ARV² 429.26) and other late archaic vases surveyed by D. Williams, "Ajax, Odysseus, and the Arms of Achilles," *Antike Kunst* 23 (1980): 137–145 with plates (see also O. Touchefeu in *LIMC* I.1, *s.v.* "Aias I," 325–327). Most of them also display the initial στάσις in lively fashion.

The third and final variant is most fully conveyed by Σ HQV *Odyssey* xi 547. Here we are told that Agamemnon shifted responsibility for the invidious decision onto some Trojan prisoners; they had been asked which of the two heroes had harmed them most, and they replied, "Odysseus." For other late witnesses to this story see Vian, Budé text of Quintus Smyrnaeus ii.9n2, Finglass's commentary on Sophocles' *Ajax*. On the contaminating account of Quintus Smyrnaeus V 1, see Vian, Budé text, ii.9–10.

Robert[46] (*Heldensage* 221) attributed the second of these versions to the *Aethiopis* ("diese einfache Fassung sind wir nun wohl berechtigt auch für die älteste zu halten und für die *Aithiopis* vorauszusetzen"). The majority of scholars, however,[47] have preferred to suppose that it is the third version which derived from our epic: see in particular Severyns (1928:331), followed by Vian, Budé text of Quintus Smyrnaeus ii.8–9, and Williams (1980:142n41). *Odyssey* xi 547 describes the judgment over the arms of Achilles in lapidary fashion: παῖδες δὲ Τρώων δίκασαν καὶ Παλλὰς Ἀθήνη. This is probably to be interpreted in the way that Σ H *ad loc.* takes it: οἱ φονευθέντες ὑπὸ Ὀδυσσέως ὅτε Αἴας τὸ πτῶμα Ἀχιλλέως ἐβάσταζεν. In other words, παῖδες Τρώων will be a mere periphrasis for "Trojans" (on the idiom involved see R. Renehan, *Greek Lexicographical Notes* [*Hypomnemata* 45 (1975)] 156–157).

Severyns supposes the third version to be a fairly straightforward attempt at explaining the apparent paradox of how the Trojans of all people came to have a say in the awarding of Achilles' arms, while the *Ilias Parva*'s account represents a more evolved (and involved) solution of the same riddle, in which the παῖδες are perversely taken to be young girls. Robert is certainly right to say that the second version of the adjudication is the simplest and therefore likely to be the oldest. But it does not follow that the oldest account is the *Aethiopis*'s. Williams

---

of the Americal Philological Association 82 [1951]: 15n23; C. P. Segal, "Pebbles in Golden Urns: The Date and Style of Corinna," *Eranos* 73 [1975]: 6; *contra* C. Carey, "Pindar's Eighth Nemean Ode," *Proceedings of the Cambridge Philological Society* 22 [1976]: 31: cf. Köhnken, *Die Funktion des Mythos bei Pindar* [Berlin 1971] 27n29) are probably an *ad hoc* invention of Pindar or Sophocles (or both) to fit their contexts; see M. C. van der Kolf, *Quaeritur quo modo Pindarus fabulas trataverit quidque in eius mutarit* (Rotterdam 1923) 66–67.

[46] Followed by P. Girard, "Comment a du se former l'*Iliade*," *Révue des Études Grecques* 15 (1902): 255, and van der Kolf, *Quaeritur quo modo Pindarus fabulas tractaverit*, 66.

[47] So Welcker, 2:177–178; Fleischer, in Roscher 1.126.10–18; Rossbach, *RE* 1 (1894): 933–934, etc.

(1980:142) points out that we cannot categorically exclude the eventuality that a Greek vote followed an initial verdict from Trojan captives or Trojan maidens, but such a scheme seems unnecessarily elaborate.

It still seems probable that the tradition that Trojan prisoners adjudged the dispute occurred in the *Aethiopis*. Probable but not proved: Jebb (commentary on Sophocles' *Ajax* [1896] xv) and Monro (commentary on the *Odyssey* 2 [1901] 359) are mistaken in supposing that the phrase ἡ ἱστορία ἐκ τῶν Κυκλίκων in Σ HQV *Odyssey* xi 547 refers forward to the following story of Agamemnon and the Trojan captives.[48] It rather refers back to the preceding words οἱ φονευθέντες ὑπὸ Ὀδυσσέως ὅτε Αἴας τὸ πτῶμα Ἀχιλλέως ἐβάσταζεν.

These most probably allude to the version of events in the *Ilias Parva*, since they fit the sentiments expressed by the second Trojan girl in F2 of that epic, where Odysseus' achievement is preferred to Ajax's.

[48] Monro is doubly wrong, since he presumes that, in the version which he takes the *Aethiopis* to have followed, "Athene herself acted as a dicast—as she did in the equally famous trial-scene of the *Eumenides*." Athena's role is only mentioned at *Odyssey* xi 547, and even there, as Jebb observed, "the poet need not be understood as conceiving that she actually presided over the award ... but merely that she influenced the minds of the arbiters." The same holds true of the vases mentioned above. Compare the goddess' rôle in *Ilias Parva* F2.

Chapter 4

Commentary on the "Fragments" of the *Aethiopis*

F1

ὁ γὰρ τὴν Αἰθιοπίδα γράφων περὶ τὸν ὄρθρον φησὶ τὸν Αἴαντα ἑαυτὸν
ἀνελεῖν.

The author of the *Aethiopis* says that Ajax killed himself around the
time of dawn.

Σ Pindar Isthmian IV 58b

Severyns (1928:325) suggests that the ultimate source of this fragment is Aristarchus himself, who seems elsewhere to have used the Epic Cycle to illustrate
Pindar (compare his citation of *Cypria* F13 apropos of *Nemean* X).

It is rather piquant that the sole fragment of our poem which is more or less
securely attested lies outside the limits of Proclus' epitome. But there is nothing
suspicious in that: Proclus' summary is deliberately curtailed, and it is unthinkable that the original poem, having described the outbreak of the quarrel over
Achilles' arms, could have failed to show its sequel, the death of Ajax.

Bethe in his note on this fragment (1922:169) shrewdly observed that
Pindar's location of Ajax's suicide ὀρθρίαι ἐν νυκτί would have corresponded to
the meaning of ὄρθρος in his own time (and perhaps the time of Homer and the
author of the *Aethiopis*), for it then referred to the last part of the night, when the
illumination of lamps and torches was still required. At a later stage of the Greek
language, however, ὄρθρος came to signify the early morning, the dawn. This is
what the word will have meant for Aristarchus and the author of our scholion,
hence the uncertainty of the latter's gloss upon the relevant Pindaric phrase.[1]

---

[1] For a fuller account of this shift in the meaning of ὄρθρος see J. Wackernagel, *Sprachliche Unter-*
suchungen zu Homer (Göttingen 1916) 193. Cf. S D. Olsen's commentary on Aristophanes *Achar-*
nians, lines 254–256.

Mention of the *Aethiopis*'s representation of Ajax's suicide[2] naturally leads to the question of whether Ajax featured as invulnerable in that poem, but this is even harder to answer than the analogous problem concerning Achilles (see page 69 above). As with the greater hero, Homer says nothing of his resistance to wounding, indeed positively denies it on two occasions.

> Αἴαντος δὲ πρῶτος ἀκόντισε φαίδιμος Ἕκτωρ
> ἔγχει, ἐπεὶ τέτραπτο πρὸς ἰθύ οἱ, οὐδ' ἀφάμαρτε,
> τῆι ῥα δύω τελαμῶνε περὶ στήθεσσι τετάσθην,
> ἤτοι ὃ μὲν σάκεος, ὃ δὲ φασγάνου ἀργυροήλου·
> τώ οἱ ῥυσάσθην τέρενα χρόα.

Iliad XIV 402–406

At *Iliad* XXIII 822–823, the duel between Ajax and Diomedes is interrupted because τότε δή ῥ' Αἴαντι περιδείσαντες Ἀχαιοὶ | παυσαμένους ἐκέλευσαν ἄεθλια ἶσ' ἀνελέσθαι, a fact noted by ancient commentators *ad locc.* (for the scholia see Erbse's edition 3.661–662 and 5.493: Eustathius also observes this [934.43 (3.479 Van der Valk], 995.1–3 (3.670 Van der Valk), 1331.29]); cf. Severyns 1928:326.

The first explicit mention of Ajax's invulnerability is in Aeschylus' Θρῆισσαι (*TrGF* 3 F83 [Radt] = Σ Sophocles *Ajax* 833 [p. 190 Christodoulou]). But for reasons already considered a propos of Achilles (page 68 above), it would be dangerous automatically to assume that the *Iliad*'s omission of this motif is due to ignorance rather than conscious suppression, or to suppose that Aeschylus invented this detail. The lateness of the feature is lengthily maintained by Berthold in his work on *Die Unverwundbarkeit in Sage und Aberglauben der Griechen* (*Religionsgeschichtliche Versuche und Vorarbeiten* 11 [1911]) 6–17, which gives a full survey of the relevant references in ancient literature. A crucial pair of texts is Hesiod fr. 250 MW and Pindar *Isthmian* VI 36–38 (our source for the former is a scholion upon line 53 of the latter [3.255 Dr.]). Berthold argued in great detail (24) what Wilamowitz reasserted with characteristic pungency (*Pindaros* [Berlin 1922], 183); that *Isthmian* VI describes a visit by Heracles to Telamon *before* the birth of Ajax (see further P. Von der Mühll, "Bemerkungen zu Pindars Nemeen und Isthmien," *Museum Helveticum* 14 [1957]: 130 = *Ausgewählte kleine Schriften* [Basel 1976] 198), so that the lionskin of Heracles as mentioned by Pindar has no connection with the tradition of Ajax's invulnerability. The scholion, misinterpreting Pindar's ἐν ῥινῶι λέοντος (line 53) as referring to a Heracles mysteriously standing *upon* his

---

[2] For artistic depictions of this see *LIMC* I.1, s.v. "Aias I," 274–276 and S. Laser, *Medizin und Körperpflege* (*Archaeologia Homerica* 20 [1983]) 78–84. See further I. Jenkins, "The Earliest Representation in Greek Art of the Death of Ajax," in *Essays in Honor of Dietrich von Bothmer* (ed. A. J. Clark and J. Gaunt) (Amsterdam 2005) 1:133–136.

lionskin (rather than standing *clad in* it), not surprisingly fails to comprehend what is happening in the poem it is commenting upon. This mistake is so readily explicable in itself that we need not take seriously Berthold's slightly divergent suggestion that the scholion was misled in its interpretation of Pindar's words by what was related in the Μεγάλαι ᾽Ηοῖαι. And indeed one further consideration provides an additional argument against this last idea. For when the scholion describes Hesiod's Heracles as ἐμβαίνων what it really means (and perhaps once said) must be ἐμβά(λ)λων τῆι δορᾶι, as J. Schwartz suggests (*Pseudo-Hesiodeia* [Leiden 1960] 391n6), comparing Σ AB *Iliad* XXIII 821 (ἀναλαβὼν τὸν παῖδα [*scil.* ᾽Ηρακλῆς] περιέβαλε τῆι λεονῆι).

This situation, then, is already more complex than Berthold allowed. No one will dispute that the *Isthmian's* myth refers to an event before Heracles' birth, or that the scholion has misunderstood Pindar's reference to the hero's lion pelt (facts accepted by, for instance, Thummer in his commentary on the relevant victory ode [p. 106] and Merkelbach–West on Hesiod fr. 250 [p. 122]). But it seems likely that the Hesiodic work already represented Heracles as wrapping the infant Ajax in his lion's hide, and it is hard to see why he should have wished to do this unless from the motive not explicitly attested until Lycophron 455–456: to render the young hero invulnerable in every area touched by the beast's pelt. Some such process is clearly presupposed by Aeschylus fr. 83 Radt = Σ Sophocles *Ajax* 833 (p. 190 Christodoulou): φησὶ δὲ περὶ αὐτοῦ Αἰσχύλος ὅτι καὶ τό ξίφος ἐκάμπτετο οὐδαμῆι ἐνδιδόντος τοῦ χρωτὸς τῆι σφαγῆι. τόξον ὥς τις ἐντείνων, κτλ. It may even, indeed, be presupposed by the prayer which Pindar puts into Heracles' mouth at *Isthmian* VI 47–48: τὸν μὲν ἄρρηκτον φυάν, ὥσπερ τόδε δέρμα με νῦν περίπλανᾶται | θηρός. As represented by Pindar, the story is not one of invulnerability magically conferred by this skin, but to say with Wilamowitz (*Pindaros*, 183) that the tradition of Ajax' invulnerability "hat mit Pindar nichts zu tun" is to underestimate the degree to which that tradition seems to peep through the significant concept of the animal hide surrounding the hero and the significant and suggestive phrase ἄρρηκτον φυάν. It is also to overlook the frequency with which Pindar, when rewriting the contents of a myth, will allow one or two vestigial features of the original version to remain (the λέβης and ivory shoulder blade of Pelops in *Olympian* I 46–51, the σκόπος of Apollo in *Pythian* III 27, etc.).

In other words, Hesiod fr. 250 MW, when rightly understood, is valuable evidence that, far from Lycophron 455–456 being a derivation and development from Pindar's sixth *Isthmian* (as Berthold and numerous others have supposed), Pindar's poem presupposes the tradition preserved in Lycophron. This fits perfectly with the deductions which, quite independently, we drew above from Aeschylus' Θρῆισσαι (*TrGF* 3 F83 Radt).

These findings cast an interesting light on Berthold's insistence that the apparent lateness of the lionskin story is fully in keeping with the actual lateness of the motif's application to Ajax. If invulnerability is to be transferred by process of sympathetic magic from hide to child, the lion's pelt must first have been impenetrable, and Berthold (*Unverwundbarkeit*, 2) supposes himself to have proved in turn that that tradition is later than the sixth century. Moreover, Heracles' encounter with the infant Ajax occurs in the context of his expedition against Troy, and the lateness of the tradition of the first Trojan War has been strongly urged by several scholars in addition to Berthold. But the agreement between Pindar (*Olympian* VIII 45, *Isthmian* V 35–37, fr. 172 Sn.) and Euripides (*Andromache* 796) over the detail of Peleus' participation in the first sack of Troy has suggested to Vian (on Quintus Smyrnaeus I 503–505 [Budé i.32n1]) that this tradition already appeared in the *Aethiopis*.

If these suggestions of lateness are not amply counterbalanced by our above analysis of the evidence of "Hesiod" and Pindar and Aeschylus, they will, I feel, be completely outweighed when we come to the following considerations, which fall into two categories: the general and the specific. Under the former heading we may recall how, when considering the parallel case of Achilles (page 70 above) we saw that the motif of a hero's invulnerability appears to be widely disseminated and primitive. Supposing that Ajax was originally conceived as a giant (a suggestion favored by several scholars,[3] most notably Von der Mühll, *Der grosse Aias* [Basel 1930] = *Ausgewählte kleine Schriften* [Basel 1975] 435), it would be totally appropriate for invulnerability to have been associated with him from the start: compare the position of the Giants in Apollodorus *Epitome* 1.35 (6.4), where they cannot be killed by the gods.

Turning from the general to the specific, we may first adduce an argument already advanced by Severyns (1928:326–327). Apollodorus *Epitome* 5.4 (considered page 71 above), with its picture of Ajax carrying back Achilles' corpse to the ships under a hail of enemy darts (Αἴας βαλλόμενος βέλεσι μέσον τῶν πολεμίων), might be thought to indicate that the *Aethiopis* depicted this hero as invulnerable. Likewise, the evidence of art. At least an Etruscan statuette of bronze dateable to the second quarter of the fifth century (Basel Kä 531: *LIMC* I.1, *s.v.* "Aias I," no. 133: see Figure 9) and a cup by the Brygos Painter from the first quarter (J. Paul Getty Museum, Malibu 86.AE.286 [formerly New York, Metropolitan Museum of Art L.69-11.35]: *Paralipomena* 367.1; *LIMC* I.1, *s.v.* "Aias I,"

---

[3] As appropriate for a giant-like being as the other main version of Ajax's decease, which we find in Σ *Iliad* XIV 405 (3.662 Erbse) and *hypothesis*, Sophocles *Ajax* (pp. 10.54–55 Christodoulou; cf. Sophron fr. 31 KA). See my remarks in *Crime and Punishment in Homeric and Archaic Epic* (Ithaca 2014) 224–225.

Figure 9. Etruscan bronze figurine (cista handle): the suicide of Ajax, with sword piercing underneath his left arm. Second quarter of the 5th century BCE. Once on loan to the Antikenmuseum Basel, Kä 531; now reverted to private collection. Drawing by Valerie Woelfel.

no. 140: see Figure 10) variously indicate a sword wound under the left armpit in a manner thoroughly compatible with Aeschylus fr. 83 Radt discussed *above;* see the discussions by M. I. Davies, "The Suicide of Ajax: A Bronze Etruscan Statuette from the Käppeli Collection," *Antike Kunst* 14 (1971): 153–154 and pl. 48.2; and Davies, "Ajax and Tekmessa," *Antike Kunst* 16 (1973): 60 and pl. 9.1.

Also, an Etruscan mirror in Boston (99.494: *LIMC s.v.* "Aias 1," no. 135; bibliography and illustration in M. I. Davies, "Suicide of Ajax," 154n3 and pl. 48.3) dateable ca. 380, shows (to quote J. D. Beazley, "The World of the Etruscan Mirror," *Journal of Hellenic Studies* 69 [1949]: 8), "a unique representation of the Death of Ajax," who "kneels with a crumpled sword in his left hand and looks round wildly at *Menerva,* who hastens towards him." The similarity to the Aeschylean fr. is patent, but Beazley concludes, "The design on the mirror is probably derived from the epic source which Aeschylus used; and in this it would seem to have been Athena who indicated the vulnerable place" (compare his remarks in *Etruscan Vase Painting* [Oxford 1947] 140 and n1). Furthermore, both the Iliadic scholia and Eustathius (cited page 84 above) presuppose an Aristarchean note (van Thiel 2014:2.508), contrasting the version of οἱ νεώτεροι (including the *Aethiopis* poet) with Homer's presentation of a woundable Ajax: compare Σ Gen. *Iliad* XIV 406 (1.176 Nicole): παραδίδωσιν τρωτὸν αὐτὸν ὁ ποιητής, καὶ οὐχ ὡς οἱ νεώτεροι, αὐτὸν ἱστοροῦσιν ἄτρωτον.

Figure 10. Red-figure cup: interior, death of Ajax,
with sword piercing his left side. Attributed to the Brygos Painter, ca. first
quarter of the 5th century BCE. Malibu, CA, J. Paul Getty Museum 86.EA.286.
Photo courtesy of the Getty's Open Content Program.

Severyns' guess that the *Aethiopis*' Ajax was invulnerable[4] may be right, then. I cannot believe, however, in his particular formulation of the motif's history. He distinguishes four stages:

- Homer (where Ajax is distinctly vulnerable)
- Hesiod fr. 250 MW
- Pindar *Isthmian* [he mistakenly refers to this as *Nemean*] VI 47 and fr. 261 Sn.
- Finally, Aeschylus fr. 83 Radt, where Ajax's single vulnerable spot represents a late attempt to reconcile the two earlier variant traditions of invulnerability and suicide.

But we have already seen that the whole question is far too complex to be reduced to this kind of facile schematization. We have also seen that Pindar and the Hesiodic fragment probably presuppose the tradition of invulnerability (the Pindaric "fragment," like Σ *Isthmian* VI 53, is merely a misunderstanding of Pindar's reference to Heracles' lionskin).

---

[4]   It is followed by, for instance, Vian in his Budé text of Quintus Smyrnaeus (i.163).

A new (and final) point to establish here is that there was surely never a version wherein Ajax was *completely* invulnerable and unkillable. By definition, all invulnerable heroes are invulnerable *except in one spot*. This is a feature essential to the significance of the motif (cf. J. Th. Kakridis, "Caeneus," *Classical Review* 61 [1947]: 79–80), and the one vulnerable spot must always have formed part of the invulnerability tradition. Various sources variously locate this deadly region: the neck is mentioned by Σ A *Iliad* XIV 406 (3.661 Erbse); it was the armpit, according to Aeschylus fr. 83 Radt (*ap.* Σ *Iliad loc. cit.*) and the two artifacts considered above. Sophocles *Ajax* 834 has its hero plunge the sword into his πλευρά, without (as Σ *ad loc.* observes) saying why. Which if any of these possibilities the *Aethiopis* employed we can hardly know. But Severyns' idea that Ajax was totally invulnerable is hardly reconcilable with F1's statement that Ajax committed suicide in the poem.

F2

["τίς πόθεν εἰς] σύ, γύναι; τίνος ἔκγον[ος]
εὔχ[ε]αι εἶναι;"

"Who are you, lady, and from where, and whose offspring
do you claim to be?

P.Oxy. XIII 1611 fr. 4 ii 145

These fragments come from what Grenfell and Hunt in their *editio princeps* (*Oxyrhynchus Papyri* XIII (London 1919): 127–128) called "a work on literary criticism." The same work is the source for Chamaeleon's treatment of the disputed authorship of Stesichorus fr. 270 Davies and Finglass = Lamprocles fr. 735 P = Chamaeleon fr. 29^c (9^2.56) Wehrli.

Allen's supplements were quoted in the *editio princeps*. The derivation from the *Aethiopis* has been found plausible by, for instance, Vian on Quintus Smyrnaeus I 551–562 (i.33n3), although the *editio princeps* itself admits that "the colour of frg. 3 and 4 is different, so that a connexion between them is unlikely" (p. 145).

On the principle of word-division that makes the introduction of Arctinus' name in fr. 4ii.149 even more difficult see E. G. Turner, *Greek Manuscripts of the Ancient World* (Oxford 1971) 19–20 and n3.

On Allen's interpretation, the hexameter σύ, γύναι, etc., will be spoken to Penthesileia by Achilles (see Grenfell-Hunt, p. 146), a possibility which Vian takes to entail that Achilles spoke first in their encounter, the reverse of what happens in Quintus Smyrnaeus I 551–562. For ἔκγονος as the correct spelling see Barrett on Euripides *Hippolytus* 447; West, "Miscellaneous Notes on the *Works and Days*," *Philologus* 108 (1964): 167. West (2013:139) notes Priam's initial greeting to Penthesileia as another possibility.

Chapter 4

Fragmentum Spurium

> ὡς οἵ γ᾽ ἀμφίεπον τάφον Ἕκτορος· ἦλθε δ᾽ Ἀμαζών,
> Ἄρηος θυγάτηρ μεγαλήτορος ἀνδροφόνοιο.

> So they busied themselves about the funeral of Hector. And there
>   came an Amazon,
> daughter of Ares the great-hearted and man-slaying god.

Σ T Iliad XXIV 804a

For a brief bibliography of treatments of the numerous problems posed by these two lines see Erbse's note on the scholion which preserves them and West 2013: 136–137. Many may be surprised not to find these two verses registered here as "*Aethiopis* fr. 1." We must therefore remind ourselves, right at the start, that the scholion says nothing to support the once-popular modern assumptions that these lines represent either the start of the *Aethiopis*[5] or an attempt to fasten that epic to the end of the *Iliad*. On the contrary, it merely reports the existence of a variant reading consisting of these two lines. Now if this reading could be shown to be superior to that of the manuscripts of the *Iliad*, then the possibility of a fragment of the *Aethiopis* could be quite definitely excluded. We must begin, therefore, by considering that possibility, however remote it may seem.

The only scholar to have seriously argued it is Eduard Meyer, "Die Rhapsoden und die Homerischen Epen," *Hermes* 53 (1918): 333, who supposes that the two hexameters at issue represent the original ending of the poem. For the "superficial transition" from one subject to another he compares the start of *Iliad* XXIII (ὡς οἱ μὲν στενάχοντο κατὰ πτόλιν· αὐτὰρ Ἀχαιοὶ) with the following passages:

> ὡς οἱ μὲν τοιαῦτα πρὸς ἀλλήλους ἀγόρευον,
> δαιτυμόνες δ᾽ ἐς δώματ᾽ ἴσαν θείου βασιλῆος....
> ὡς οἱ μὲν περὶ δεῖπνον ἐνὶ μεγάροισι πένοντο.
> μνηστῆρες δὲ πάροιθεν Ὀδυσσῆος μεγάροιο ...

Odyssey iv 620–625

---

5 Wilamowitz, *Homerische Untersuchungen* (Berlin 1884) 373 on the relevant verse: "den keine überlieferung, sondern nur moderne willkür für den anfang der Aithiopis ausgibt." This assumption was given respectability by Welcker (1:199) and is taken seriously as recently as Solmsen, "The Conclusion to the *Odyssey*," in *Poetry and Poetics from Ancient Greece to the Renaissance*, ed. G. M. Kirkwood (Ithaca, NY 1975) 15 = *Kleine Schriften* 3.3.

ὥς οἱ μὲν Τρῶες φυλακὰς ἔχον· αὐτὰρ Ἀχαιούς
θεσπεσίη ἔχε φύζα ...

Iliad IX 1–2

ὥς ὁ μὲν ἐν κλισίηισι Μενοιτίου ἄλκιμος υἱός
ἰᾶτ' Εὐρύπυλον βεβλημένον· οἱ δ' ἐμάχοντο
Ἀργεῖοι, καὶ Τρῶες ὁμιλαδόν.

Iliad XII 1–3

ὥς ὁ μὲν ἔνθα καθεῦδε πολύτλας δῖος Ὀδυσσεύς
ὕπνωι καὶ καμάτωι ἀρημένος· αὐτὰρ Ἀθήνη
βῆ ῥ' ἐς Φαιήκων ἀνδρῶν δῆμόν τε πόλιν τε.

Odyssey vi 1–3

ὥς ὁ μὲν ἔνθ' ἠρᾶτο πολύτλας δῖος Ὀδυσσεύς,
κούρην δὲ προτὶ ἄστυ φέρεν μένος ἡμιόνοιϊν.

Odyssey vii 1–2

οἱ μέν ῥ' εὔχοντο Ποσειδάωνι ἄνακτι,
δήμου Φαιήκων ἡγήτορες ἠδὲ μέδοντες,
ἑσταότες περὶ βωμόν· ὁ δ' ἔγρετο δῖος Ὀδυσσεύς.

Odyssey xiii 185–187

Even if these parallels worked on the merely formal level, we would have to conclude that some of them are singularly ill-chosen. *Odyssey* iv 620–625 has often been taken to show signs of textual mutilation (see, for instance, D. L. Page, *The Homeric Odyssey* [Oxford 1955] 69 and 80n15) and on *Odyssey* xiii 187 Focke 1951:272–274.

As it is, none of their transitions exhibits anything like the abruptness—either in rhythm or content—of the change of subject in our two lines. But fully to combat the implications about the *Iliad*'s composition contained in Meyer's suggestion that the final rhapsodes responsible for the poem deliberately created connections with the *Aethiopis* and *Iliupersis* in its closing sections,[6] and that the very last specimen of such links was abruptly severed to create an artificial internal unity, would require more time and space than I can here dispose of. I may merely remark how unlikely it is that the original ending of the poem should have come so close to total disappearance, preserved from oblivion by the slender thread of a *varia lectio*.

---

[6] For such forward-looking references in *Iliad* XXIII, see, for instance, Willcock 1973; for the like in *Iliad* XXIV, P. Von der Mühll, *Kritisches Hypomnema zur Ilias* (Basil 1952) 370.

And as we shall see, the phrase Ἄρηος ... μεγαλήτορος in the allegedly original ending is in truth indicative of a post-Homeric origin for these lines, as is the singularly abrupt rhythm of ἦλθε δ' Ἀμάζων (see my commentary *ad loc.* in each case). Not that we need go as far as August Fick (*Die Homerische* Ilias [Göttingen 1886] 235; followed by West [2013:136–137], with references to his earlier expositions of this view), who deleted line 804 as it stands in our manuscripts on the ground that it came from the continuation into the *Aethiopis*. No: it looks rather as if, on the contrary, the alleged continuation derives from line 804, which occurs in all of our manuscripts and in its undoctored form has nothing to do with the *Aethiopis*.

But if these hexameters do not, in their reported form, belong to the end of the *Iliad*, neither do they come from the start of the *Aethiopis*. It is inconceivable that the latter epic should have begun so abruptly, without benefit of introductory proem or appeal to the Muses, and burdened with an indeterminate and irrelevant reference to the funeral of Hector: ὡς οἵ γ' hardly compares, for vivacity or point, with the first words of the *Iliad* and the *Odyssey*, or even the *Ilias Parva*, and will have provided a very eccentric substitute for a title (see Davies and Finglass on Stesichorus fr. 99). Allen's apparently unobjectionable comment *ad loc.* (p. 126)—"his versibus incepisse *Aethiopidem* ut veri simile sit ita incertum est"—proceeds, in fact, far beyond—and in the opposite direction to—the available evidence, as does Focke's verdict that "der Eingangsverse der Amazonie ist bekanntlich in den leteten Iliasvers eingehakt" (1951:226).

Kopff (*ANRW* II.31.2:930–931) deduces from the Homeric cups considered above (page 41) that the *Aethiopis* contained near its start Priam's supplication of "an Achilles who was mutilating Hector's corpse by dragging it around the walls of Troy" and suggests that the poem's transition from this topic to Penthesileia's arrival was accomplished in the two verses that are causing us so much trouble. But he himself confesses that "this reconstruction is not based on much evidence" (930), and this remark in fact constitutes an understatement.

If the distich belongs neither to the *Iliad* nor to the *Aethiopis* there is little scope for speculation. The two verses have been variously assessed as a "kyklische Verbindung zur *Aethiopis*" (Von der Mühll, *Kritisches Hypomnema zur Ilias*, 390), approved by Kullmann (1960:359n2),[7] as a "secondary transition device" (Dihle 1970:43n54), and as a late atempt at providing "the story so far ..." with no relevance to the original end or beginning of either epic (W. Kranz, "Sphragis: Ichform und Namensiegel als Eingangs- und Schlußmotiv antiker Dichtung," *Rheinisches Museum* 104 [1961]: 7 = *Studien zur Antiken Literatur*

---

[7] Similarly K. Schefold in *Wort und Bild* (Munich 1979) 309: "The verse leads directly on to the *Aethiopis.*"

und ihrem Nachwirken (Heidelberg 1967) 30. But we must, I think, be a little more careful in our definition of the lines' purpose.

The hypothesis that our distich represents an attempt to link the *Aethiopis* to the *Iliad* is often bolstered up by appeals to allegedly parallel cases. Thus M. L. West, in his discussion of the end of Hesiod's *Theogony* (p. 48 and note on *Theogony* 1019–1022), places on the same level the concluding section of that poem (which effects a smooth run into the Κατάλογος γυναικῶν), the last line of the *Works and Days* (alleged by Σ *ad loc.* = Hesiod T p. 157 MW to be an introduction to the Ὀρνιθομαντεία), and our troublesome passage. By the time he came to comment upon the relevant part of the *Works and Days* he was rightly more circumspect, distinguishing more clearly between the large portion (901 onward) which he supposes to have been added at a late date to the end of the *Theogony*, the single hexameter which he now believes to be an integral part of the *Works and Days*, and our own enigmatic distich. Each instance does indeed seem to be *sui generis*. In the *Theogony*, a sizeable chunk has been attached to the end of the poem without any noticeable distortion of the original text. If West is now right to defend the authenticity of *Works and Days* 828, it obviously has no business in our discussion. And even if it (or, indeed, all of 826–828) were added to create a transition to the work on bird omens, a fixed and certain parallel with our own two lines would still not exist: we saw above that the interpolation of the whole of *Iliad* XXIV 804 is a completely implausible hypothesis; it is far more likely that the second part of that line has been rewritten and a further line appended to continue the sense created by this reworking. This process has no real analogy in either of the Hesiodic cases considered above.

Nor is it particularly close to the situation prevailing at the end of the *Odyssey*, with which it is compared by L. E. Rossi, "La fine alessandrina dell'*Odissea* e lo ζῆλος Ὁμηρικός di Apollonio Rodio," *Rivista di Filologia e di Istruzione Classica* 96 (1968): 153n5, who follows Meyer ("Die Rhapsoden und die Homerischen Epen" [as cited above, page 90]). In *Odyssey* xxiii 295 it is a matter of the alleged replacement of an original οἱ δ᾽ ἄρ᾽ ἔπειτα[8] by the οἱ μὲν ἔπειτα which now stands in all manuscripts, and the addition after line 296 of a vast "Continuation" (exceeding six hundred lines) whose probable purpose is not to connect *Odyssey* to *Telegony* but, on the contrary, to obviate any such link. Once more, the similarity with our problem is not very plain.

Finally, the alternative (allegedly "cyclic") proem to the *Iliad*, which substitutes for that epic's original invocation a briefer and more business-like appeal to the Muses (see West's app. crit. *ad loc.*) cannot really be compared·, this

---

[8]   So A. Kirchhoff, *Die homerische Odyssee* (Berlin 1879).

prelude merely replaces the original passage with a more summary version of the same ideas. No rewriting is involved.

The total failure to produce an analogy for our two lines is not so disastrously negative as it may at first seem. For we may at least deduce that, however we choose to view them, their claim to be any sort of fragment of the *Aethiopis* must be disallowed. Suppose an interpretation of them as some sort of link between that work and the *Iliad* is the least unsatisfactory possibility at our disposal:[9] one consequence in particular follows for our lost epic: there is still no reason why a single word of either hexameter should come from the *Aethiopis*, any more than scholars ever suppose that Hesiod *Theogony* 901–1022 or *Odyssey* xxiii 297 until the end of the poem derive verbatim from the poems with which they are variously connected. On the contrary, an introductory or linking passage is hardly fulfilling its function satisfactorily if it anticipates thoughts or words from the work to which it is leading up.

The appearance of a variant version of the second line in the superficial outline of events leading to the Trojan War contained on the papyrus cited *ad loc.* merely strengthens one's skepticism.

ἦλθε δ' Ἀμαζών |

On the abrupt rhythm see Griffin 1980:159n29.

Any abruptness in similar line-end phrases elsewhere in Homer is mitigated either by the commencement of the relevant clause earlier on in the hexameter (e.g. *Odyxssey* xiii 221: σχεδόθεν δέ οἱ ἦλθεν Ἀθήνη) or by close runover of sense (e.g. *Iliad* I 194–195: ἦλθε δ' Ἀθήνη | οὐρανόθεν) with which the present example of opposition in enjambment (Ἀμαζών | Ἄρηος θυγάτηρ) does not really compare.

Ἄρηος ... μεγαλήτορος

As Dihle has observed (1970:43n54) this epithet is not applied to Ares in either the *Iliad* or the *Odyssey*.

---

[9] The very uniqueness of this alleged link between two originally separate poems makes it difficult to decide just when the artificial connection was forged. The "cyclic" edition is one conceivable explanation, although we have already seen that no real formal parallel obtains between our problem and the allegedly "cyclic opening of the *Iliad*." Having so rigorously excluded a host of false parallels, I must not introduce any of my own. I will merely remark that a feature such as the false opening of Vergil's *Aeneid* (R. G. Austin, "*Ille ego qui quondam ...*," *Classical Quarterly* 18 [1968]: 107–115) offers a potential parallel. Monro (*Odyssey* commentary 2.357) suggests an origin for the verses not inconsistent with such a line of thought.

Ἄρηος θυγάτηρ

Cf. Vergil *Aeneid* XI 661–662: *Martia ... Penthesileia.*

Ἄρηος ... ἀνδροφόνοιο

Cf. *Iliad* IV 441. where we find Ἄρεος ἀνδροφόνοιο at the start of an hexameter (as we do in *Sibylline Oracles* 12.17 Rzach). For the same two words together at the end of a line see [Hesiod] *Shield* 98. Ares has the epithet again at Nonnus *Dionysiaca* II 308–309 (cf. XXIX 346).

θυγάτηρ μεγαλήτορος

This formula occurs in this metrical position (θ. μ. - ‿ ‿ - - |) of various heroines in *Iliad* VI 395, VIII 187; *Odyssey* vi 17, 196, 213, vii 58, xi 85.

μεγαλήτορος ἀνδροφόνοιο

Ἕκτορος ἀνδροφόνοιο is used eight times as a line ending in the *Iliad*. Compare *Odyssey* x 200 (of the Cyclops) μεγαλήτορος ἀνδροφάγοιο.

Appendix

The Tabulae Iliacae

IN DEALING WITH THE POSSIBILITY THAT ARTIFACTS such as Greek vases reflect and preserve versions of myths that feature in now-lost epics, one must sedulously avoid (as I have in chapter 2) using the word "illustration," with its host of anachronistic and misleading associations. But there does exist a body of artifacts to which that term could less misleadingly be applied. These are the so-called Tabulae Iliacae, miniature marble reliefs from the early Roman Empire, inscribed in Greek and purporting to convey the contents of various early Greek narrative poems, both preserved and lost. The most useful and recent treatment of them, with a full survey of previous studies, is by Michael Squire: *The* Iliad *in a Nutshell: Visualizing Epic on the Tabulae Iliacae* (Oxford 2011); this work was not available to M. L. West when he published *The Epic Cycle* (Oxford 2013). Note also D. Petrain, *Homer in Stone: The Tabulae Iliacae in Their Roman Context* (Cambridge 2014), particularly useful for its comparison of the tables' narratives (pp. 78–88). The brute facts about the pieces, their provenance, size, state of preservation, and the like are clearly and compendiously set out by Squire for the Tabula Capitolina (1A: pp. 387–390), the Tabula Thierry (7Ti: pp. 397–398), the Tabula Veronensis II (9D: pp. 399–400), and the Tabula Froehner I (20Par: pp. 409–410). These are the reliefs that concern us here, since they represent—or once did, for some are fragmentary—scenes from the *Aethiopis*. For a handy tabular summary of the contents of each, see Petrain, p. 114.

The Tabula Capitolina is the most important (Figure A1), providing as it does the most detail in both depictions and labeling. The piece is even more crucial (and also controversial) for its central area, which notoriously claims to represent the sack of Troy κατὰ Στησίχορον. For the most recent assessment and approbation of this claim see Davies and Finglass, *The Poems of Stesichorus* on fr. 105. What concerns us here, however, is the higher of the two horizontal friezes below and to the right, where inscriptions running above and content underneath leave no doubt that we have scenes from the *Aethiopis*, although some of the detail is very indistinct. For a fuller description see Petrain, pp.

Figure A1. Tabula Capitolina: *detail*, scenes from the *Aethiopis*.
Rome, Musei Capitolini, Sala delle Columbe, inv. MC316/S. *Above*: photo, Archivio Fotografico dei Musei Capitolini.
Below: drawing by Louis Schulz, in O. Jahn, *Griechische Bilderchroniken* (Bonn 1873), Tafel I*.

Figure A2. Tabula Thierry (*lost*).
Photo, O. Rayet, "Note sur un fragment inédit de table iliaque du Cabinet de
M. Thierry," in *Mémoires de la Société des Antiquaires de France* 43:17–23.

198–199. From left to right there are, after an initial panel now illegible because
it is fragmentary, the following:

- Achilles killing Penthesileia, who falls towards him. Tower of Troy
  in background.
- Achilles killing Thersites by raising a weapon, in front of a building perhaps representing Penthesileia's tomb.
- Achilles killing Memnon, with Antilochus' corpse slumped behind
  his killer, and behind that the walls of Troy.
- Next, the other side of the city, with its gate open, and Ajax raising a protective shield over a seated Achilles, who holds shield in
  similar position.
- Then, Odysseus raising his shield to protect Ajax while Achilles is
  slumped against the body of Ajax, who carries him off.
- Achilles lying with body in the hollow of his shield, over his head
  a female figure and then another (labeled as Thetis and Muse)
  and an altar.
- Finally, a seated Ajax holding his head in a presumed posture of
  despair.

The Tabula Thierry is now lost, but its recto, preserved as a heliogravure
in 1882 (Figure A2), "seems to have depicted the *Aethiopis* rather than the *Iliad*

Figure A3. Tabula Veronensis II.
Paris, Bibliothèque Nationale de France, Cabinet des Médailles, inv. 3319.
Drawing after O. Jahn, *Griechische Bilderchroniken* (Bonn 1873), Tafel III.

around its central *Ilioupersis* scene" (Squire, p. 185). Squire observes, "The *Aethiopis* scenes are difficult to make out—the inscriptions seem to have named the Amazon Penthesileia, Agamemnon, and Achilles (among others)" (p. 398). For a more detailed account see Petrain, pp. 216–217. The Tabula Veronensis II (Figure A3) shows "the *Aethiopis* scenes from top to bottom," these scenes being "also inscribed to their left, including short phrases that identify each scene" (Squire, p. 399). For a more detailed description see Petrain, pp. 220–221. The remaining tabula (Froehner I) is too fragmentary to be deciphered: see Petrain, pp. 224–225.

One particular drawing of the Tabula Capitolina is problematic in a way that requires fuller consideration. It is perhaps a little unfortunate that, in the case of the *Aethiopis* and other relevant cyclic epics, Martin West chose to reproduce the drawings of Feodor Ivanovich (and even Squire fails to give adequate warning about this). For although these drawings are much prettier than the accurate alternative, they are nevertheless, for that very reason, sometimes danger-ously inaccurate and misleading. This truth can be established by comparing the drawing by Louis Schulz for Otto Jahn here reproduced as Figure A1 with that by Ivanovich reproduced by West. I herewith proceed to supply for the author of the latter drawing some biographical details culled from W. St. Clair, *Lord Elgin and the Marbles* (London 1967), index *s.v.* "Calmuck, Theodor, Lord

Elgin's," especially p. 61, which will suggest some of the reasons for the choice of Ivanovich as draftsman, and conceivably some of the reasons for his inaccuracy, as well as providing some innocent amusement.

The drawing of the Tabula Iliaca by Feodor (or Theodor) Ivanovich (1765–1832) was first published near the end of the first quarter of the nineteenth century in J. H. W. Tischbein, *Homer nach Antiken gezeichnet* VII (Stuttgart 1821) plate 2. Its main and most obvious flaw is its exaggeratedly clear and sharp representation of what on the original, because of its small size and the surface attrition caused by centuries of burial underground, is blurred and indistinct. It has thus exercised a baleful influence over the centuries. Its author was certainly an interesting man. Born a Tartar, he was kidnapped as a child by Cossacks. He later lived at the courts of St. Petersburg and Baden and studied in Rome. He produced drawings (now in the Elgin portfolio in the British Museum) of sculptures on the Acropolis at Athens for Lord Elgin, and was thought by that worthy's secretary to be perhaps the only man of taste ever produced by his nation. So far, well. But we then read the potentially sinister words (italics mine) that "with astonishing *imagination* and good judgement, he made lively *restorations* on paper of how they *must* have looked." Consternation sets in with the news that "unfortunately ... he was extremely lazy and had an uncommon relish for strong liquor." Apparently he could only be made to work "by a judicious administration of brandy." The final nail in the coffin is supplied when we learn[1] that so good a judge as Goethe said of him "that he was a man gifted with a great deal of talent, whose clear drawings nearly always indicate taste and mind. But he had hardly sufficient knowledge and accuracy to let one look for the highest standard of truthfulness of style."[2]

After all this, it may come as an anticlimax to state the sum of our knowledge gained from these artifacts as being that they confirm the contents of Proclus' summary; but so it is.

---

[1] See A. H. Smith, "Lord Elgin and His Collection," *Journal of Hellenic Studies* 36 (1916): 172. Admittedly, this verdict is reported at second or even third hand.

[2] Petrain (p. 4n8) does warn against Ivanovitch's line drawing (it "cannot be trusted for details or for the placement of inscriptions").

Bibliography of Frequently Cited Works

Allan, W. 2005. "Arms and the Man: Euphorbus, Hector, and the Death of Patro-clus." *Classical Quarterly* 55:1–16.

Andersen, Øivind. 1978. *Die Diomedesgestalt in der Ilias. Symbolae Osloenses* Suppl. 25. Oslo.

———. 1982. "Thersites und Thoas vor Troia." *Symbolae Osloenses* 57:7–34.

Bethe, Erich. 1922. *Homer, Dichtung und Sage, 2: Odyssee. Kyklos. Zeitbestimmung nebst den resten des troischen Kyklos.* Leipzig.

von Bothmer, Dietrich. 1981. "The Death of Sarpedon." In *The Greek Vase*, ed. Stephen L. Hyatt, 63–80. Latham, NY.

Burgess, J. 2001. *The Tradition of the Trojan War in Homer and the Epic Cycle.* Baltimore.

Clark, M. E., and W. D. E. Coulson. 1978. "Memnon and Sarpedon." *Museum Helveticum* 35:62–73.

Dietrich, B. C. 1965. *Death, Fate, and the Gods: The Development of a Religious Idea in Greek Popular Belief and in Homer.* London.

Dihle, Albrecht. 1970. *Homer-Probleme.* Cologne.

Dodds, E. R. 1968. "Homer." In *Fifty Years (and Twelve) of Classical Scholarship*, ed. Maurice Platnauer, 1–13, 31–34. New York.

Fenik, Bernard. 1968. *Typical Battle Scenes in the Iliad: Studies in the Narrative Techniques of Homeric Battle Description.* Hermes Einzelschriften 21. Wiesbaden.

Focke, F. "Homerisches." *La Nouvelle Clio* 3 (1951): 335–348.

Friis Johansen, K. 1967. *The Iliad in Early Greek Art.* Copenhagen.

Griffin, Jasper. 1977. "The Epic Cycle and the Uniqueness of Homer." *Journal of Hellenic Studies* 97:39–53.

———. 1980. *Homer on Life and Death.* Oxford.

Hölscher, Uvo. 1955. Review of Schadewaldt 1952. *Gnomon* 27:385–399.

Howald, E. 1946. *Der Dichter der* Ilias. Zurich.

Kakridis, J. Th. 1949. *Homeric Researches.* Lund.

Kelly, A. 2006. "Neoanalysis and the 'Nestorbedrängnis': A Test Case." *Hermes* 134: 13–19.

Kossatz-Deissmann, A. 1981. "Nestor und Antilochus: Zu den spätarchaischen Bildern mit Leberschau." *Archäologischer Anzeiger* 96:562–576.

Kullmann, Wolfgang. 1960. *Die Quellen der* Ilias: *Troischer Sagenkreis.* Wiesbaden.

Kullmann, Wolfgang. 1977. Review of Dihle 1970. *Gnomon* 49:529–543.

———. 1981. "Zur Methode der Neoanalyse in der Homerforschung." *Wiener Studien* 15:5–42.

Lesky, Albin. 1967. *Homeros: Sonderausgaben der Paulyschen Realencyclopädie der classischen Altertumswissenschaft.* Stuttgart. [= *RE* Suppl. 11.687–846 (1968).]

Lung, G. E. 1912. *Memnon: Archäologische Studien zur* Aithiopis. Bonn.

Mayer-Prokop, I. 1967. *Die gravierten etruskischen Griffspiegel archaischen Stils* (*Mitteilungen des Deutschen Archäologischen Instituts, Römische Abteilung* Suppl. 13). Heidelberg.

Page, D. L. 1963. "Homer and the Neoanalytiker." Review of Schoeck 1961. *Classical Review* 13:21–24.

Pestalozzi, Heinrich. 1945. *Die Achilleis als Quelle der* Ilias. Erlenbach.

Reichardt, B. 2007. "Mythischer Mütter: Thetis und Eos in der attischen Bilderwelt des 6. und 5. Jhdts v. Chr." In *Besorgte Mütter und sorglose Zecher: Mythische Exempel in der Bilderwelt Athens,* ed. M. Meyer, 13–98. Vienna.

Reinhardt, Karl. 1961. *Die Ilias und ihr Dichter.* Göttingen.

Robertson, Martin. 1969. "*Geryoneis:* Stesichorus and the Vase-Painters." *Classical Quarterly* 19:207–221.

Rohde, E. 1886. *Psyche.* 9th ed. Berlin.

Rzach, A. 1922. "Kyklos." In *RE* 11.2.2347–2435.

Schadewaldt, Wolfgang. 1952. *Varia Variorum: Festgabe für K. Reinhardt.* Münster.

Schoeck, Georg. 1961. Ilias *und* Aethiopis: *Kyklische Motive in homerischer Brechung.* Zurich.

Severyns, A. 1925. "L'*Éthiopide* d'Arctinos et la question du Cycle épique." *Révue de Philologie* 49:153–183.

———. 1928. *Le cycle épique dans l'école d'Aristarque.* Paris.

Welcker, F. G. 1865. *Der epische Cyclus* (1841; 2nd ed., 2 vols., 1865). Bonn.

West, M. L. 2003. "Iliad *and* Aethiopis *on the Stage.*" *Classical Quarterly* 53:1–14. [= *Hellenica* 1: *Epic* (Oxford 2011) 242–264.]

———. 2011. *The Making of the* Iliad. Oxford.

———. 2013. *The Epic Cycle: A Commentary on the Lost Troy Epics.* Oxford.

Willcock, M. M. 1973. "The Funeral Games of Patroclus." *Bulletin of the Institute of Classical Studies* 20:1–11.

———. 1983. "Antilochus in the *Iliad.*" In *Mélanges Edouard Delebecque,* 477–485. Aix-en-Provence.

Index Nominum

Index Rerum

Aethiopis: date of, 45

Ethiopians: and their locale, 24, 59

folk-tale motifs: hero's invulnerability, 67–70, 84–89; mother brings son armor, 60

Funeral Games, 78; mourning at, 20, 74

"Grieving Mother" motif, 32

hepatoscopy, 62–63

"Homeric Cups," 42–43

Iliac tablets. *See* Tabulae Iliacae

Iliad: end tailored to fit start of *Aethiopis*, 90–95

kerostasia. *See under* souls: weighing of

Memnonis: alleged existence of, 1–2, 23–24

Neoanalysis, 3–24

Nereids: as mourners, 20, 75

pollution, 55–57

prothesis, 20, 75

Psychostasia. *See under* souls: weighing of

skin color, 59n17

souls: weighing of, 17–18, 25–31

suicide, 83

Tabulae Iliacae, 97–101

CPSIA information can be obtained
at www.ICGtesting.com
Printed in the USA
JSHW032118150822
29286JS00005B/14

9 780674 088313